Minich

Minich

THE VISUAL DICTIONARY *of the*

UNIVERSE

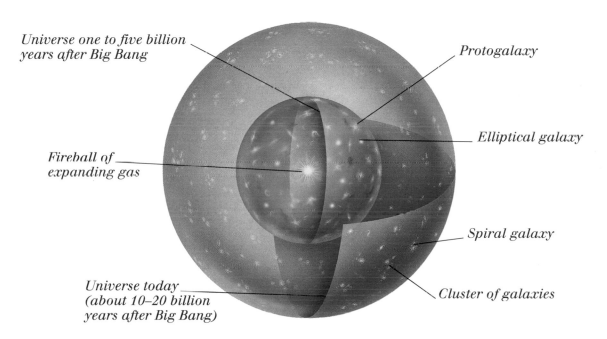

Universe one to five billion
years after Big Bang

Protogalaxy

Elliptical galaxy

Fireball of
expanding gas

Spiral galaxy

Universe today
(about 10–20 billion
years after Big Bang)

Cluster of galaxies

ORIGIN AND EXPANSION OF THE UNIVERSE

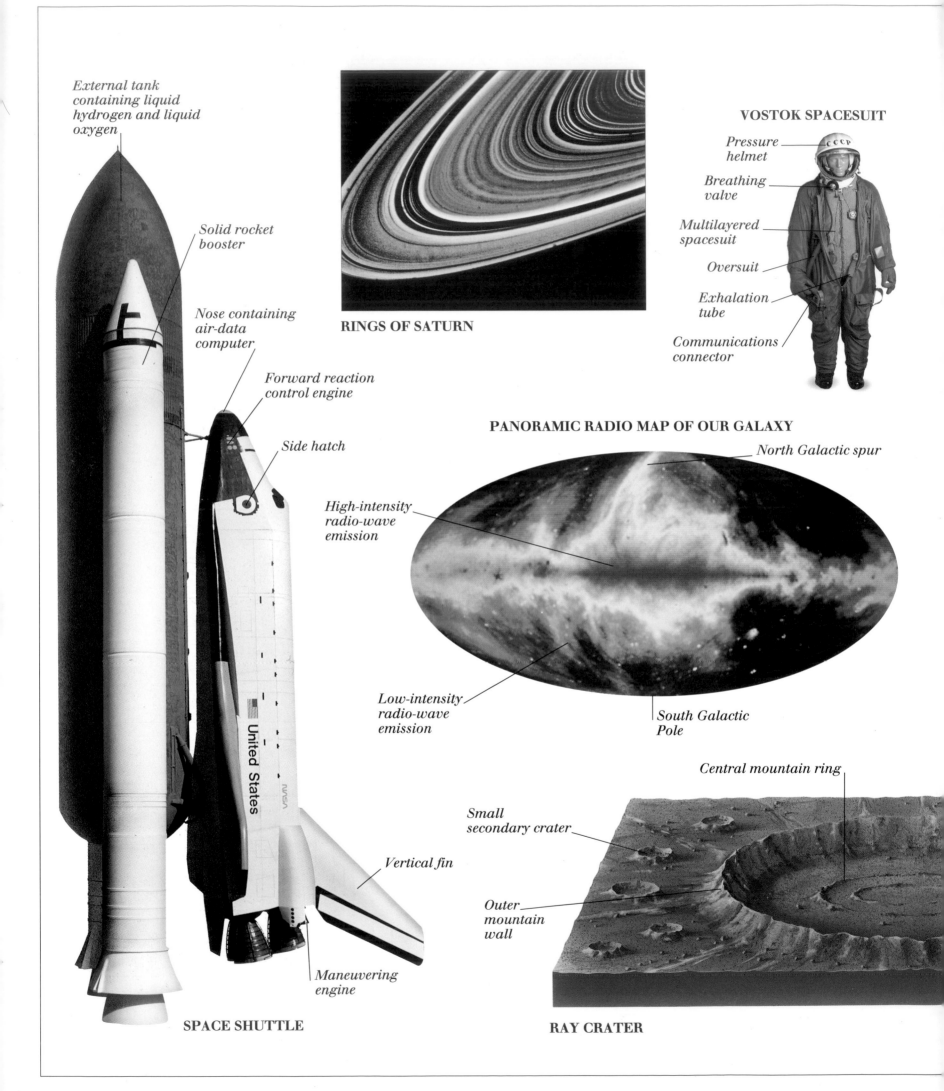

External tank
containing liquid
hydrogen and liquid
oxygen

Solid rocket
booster

Nose containing
air-data
computer

Forward reaction
control engine

Side hatch

High-intensity
radio-wave
emission

United States

Vertical fin

Maneuvering
engine

SPACE SHUTTLE

RINGS OF SATURN

VOSTOK SPACESUIT

Pressure
helmet

Breathing
valve

Multilayered
spacesuit

Oversuit

Exhalation
tube

Communications
connector

PANORAMIC RADIO MAP OF OUR GALAXY

North Galactic spur

Low-intensity
radio-wave
emission

South Galactic
Pole

Central mountain ring

Small
secondary crater

Outer
mountain
wall

RAY CRATER

EYEWITNESS VISUAL DICTIONARIES

THE VISUAL
DICTIONARY *of the*
UNIVERSE

Ascraeus Mons (volcano)

Pavonis Mons (volcano)

Valles Marineris

MARS

Ray of ejecta (ejected material)

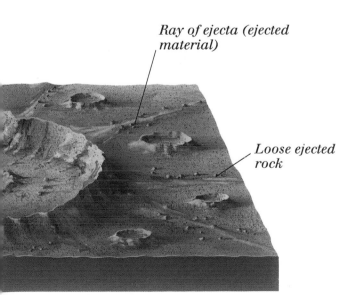

Loose ejected rock

DORLING KINDERSLEY

LONDON • NEW YORK • STUTTGART

A DORLING KINDERSLEY BOOK

PROJECT ART EDITOR DUNCAN BROWN
DESIGN ASSISTANTS SUSAN KNIGHT, ELLEN WOODWARD

PROJECT EDITOR PAUL DOCHERTY
EDITORIAL ASSISTANT EMILY HILL
ASTRONOMY CONSULTANT EDITOR SUE BECKLAKE
SPACE TECHNOLOGY CONSULTANT EDITOR KENNETH W. GATLAND
U.S. EDITOR CHARLES A. WILLS
U.S. CONSULTANT PROFESSOR WARREN YASSO

MANAGING ART EDITOR PHILIP GILDERDALE
SENIOR EDITOR MARTYN PAGE
MANAGING EDITOR RUTH MIDGLEY

PHOTOGRAPHY ANDY CRAWFORD, BOB GATHANY
ILLUSTRATIONS CHRIS LYON, JULIAN BAUM, RICK BLAKELEY, KUO KANG CHEN, MARK FRANKLIN, SELWYN HUTCHINSON
PRODUCTION JAYNE SIMPSON

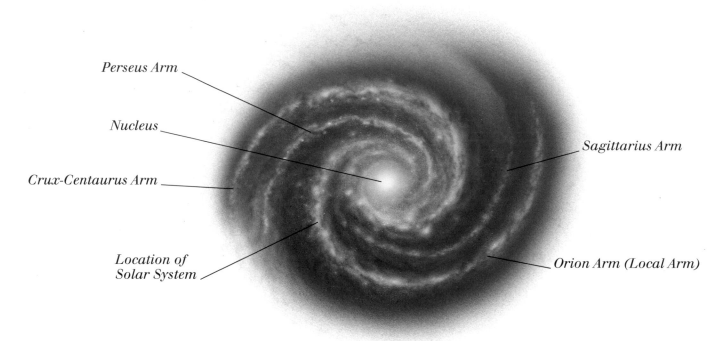

Perseus Arm

Nucleus

Crux-Centaurus Arm

Sagittarius Arm

Location of
Solar System

Orion Arm (Local Arm)

OVERHEAD VIEW OF OUR GALAXY

FIRST AMERICAN EDITION, 1993

2 4 6 8 10 9 7 5 3 1

PUBLISHED IN THE UNITED STATES BY
DORLING KINDERSLEY, INC., 232 MADISON AVENUE
NEW YORK, NEW YORK 10016

LIBRARY OF CONGRESS CATALOGING-IN-PUBLICATION DATA

THE EYEWITNESS visual dictionary of the universe. — 1ST AMERICAN ED.
p. cm. — (THE EYEWITNESS visual dictionaries)
INCLUDES INDEX.

ISBN 1–56458–336–8
1. ASTRONOMY—PICTORIAL WORKS. 2. ASTRONOMY—POPULAR WORKS.
I. DORLING KINDERSLEY LIMITED. II. SERIES.
QB68.E94 1993
520'.3—dc20   93–22419
                                                    CIP

REPRODUCED BY COLOURSCAN, SINGAPORE
PRINTED AND BOUND IN ITALY BY ARNOLDO MONDADORI, VERONA

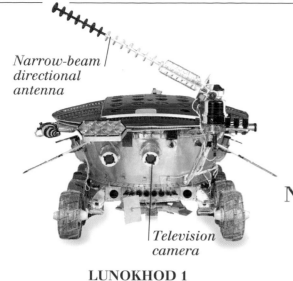

Narrow-beam directional antenna

Television camera

LUNOKHOD 1

Contents

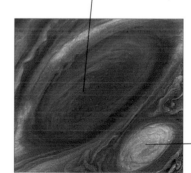

Thin, straight gas tail

Broad, curved dust tail

Coma surrounding nucleus of dust and frozen gases

STRUCTURE OF A COMET

Rings of rocks and dust

Atmosphere

Mantle

Rocky core

URANUS

Great Red Spot

White oval

CLOUD FEATURES OF JUPITER

Stone (olivine)

Iron

STONY-IRON METEORITE

Heat shield

Parachute container

Radiator

High-gain parabolic antenna

Solar panel

MARS 3 ORBITER AND LANDER

The Universe

THE UNIVERSE CONTAINS EVERYTHING that exists, from the tiniest subatomic particles to galactic superclusters (the largest structures known). Nobody knows how big the Universe is, but astronomers estimate that it contains about 100 billion galaxies, each comprising an average of 100 billion stars. The most widely accepted theory about the origin of the Universe is the Big Bang theory, which states that the Universe came into being in a huge explosion—the Big Bang—that took place between 10 and 20 billion years ago. The Universe initially consisted of a very hot, dense fireball of expanding, cooling gas. After about one million years, the gas probably began to condense into localized clumps called protogalaxies. During the next five billion years, the protogalaxies continued condensing, forming galaxies in which stars were being born. Today, billions of years later, the Universe as a whole is still expanding, although there are localized areas in which objects are held together by gravity; for example, many galaxies are found in clusters. The Big Bang theory is supported by the discovery of faint, cool background radiation coming evenly from all directions. This radiation is believed to be the remnant of the radiation produced by the Big Bang. Small "ripples" in the temperature of the cosmic background radiation are thought to be evidence of slight fluctuations in the density of the early Universe, which resulted in the formation of galaxies. Astronomers do not yet know if the Universe is "closed," which means it will eventually stop expanding and begin to contract, or if it is "open," which means it will continue expanding forever.

COMPUTER-ENHANCED MICROWAVE MAP OF COSMIC BACKGROUND RADIATION

Pale blue indicates "cool ripples" in background radiation

Pink indicates "warm ripples" in background radiation

Deep blue indicates background radiation corresponding to -454.5°F (remnant of the Big Bang)

Red and pink band indicates radiation from our galaxy

Low-energy microwave radiation corresponding to about -454°F

High-energy gamma radiation corresponding to about 5,400°F

ORIGIN AND EXPANSION OF THE UNIVERSE

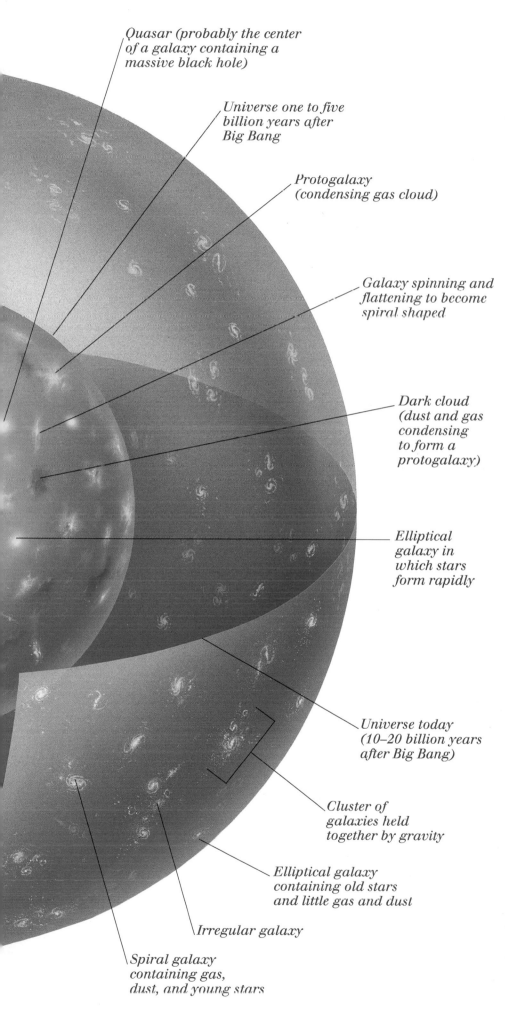

Quasar (probably the center
of a galaxy containing a
massive black hole)

Universe one to five
billion years after
Big Bang

Protogalaxy
(condensing gas cloud)

Galaxy spinning and
flattening to become
spiral shaped

Dark cloud
(dust and gas
condensing
to form a
protogalaxy)

Elliptical
galaxy in
which stars
form rapidly

Universe today
(10–20 billion years
after Big Bang)

Cluster of
galaxies held
together by gravity

Elliptical galaxy
containing old stars
and little gas and dust

Irregular galaxy

Spiral galaxy
containing gas,
dust, and young stars

OBJECTS IN THE UNIVERSE

**CLUSTER OF
GALAXIES IN VIRGO**

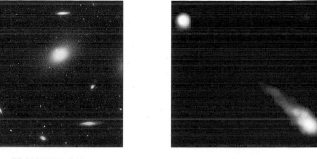

**COLOR-ENHANCED IMAGE
OF 3C273 (QUASAR)**

**NGC 4406
(ELLIPTICAL GALAXY)**

**NGC 5236
(SPIRAL GALAXY)**

**NGC 6822
(IRREGULAR GALAXY)**

**THE ROSETTE NEBULA
(EMISSION NEBULA)**

**THE JEWEL BOX
(STAR CLUSTER)**

**THE SUN
(MAIN SEQUENCE STAR)**

EARTH

THE MOON

Galaxies

SOMBRERO,
A SPIRAL GALAXY

A GALAXY IS A HUGE MASS OF STARS, nebulae, and interstellar material. The smallest galaxies contain about 100,000 stars, while the largest contain up to 3,000 billion stars. There are three main types of galaxy, classified according to their shape: elliptical, which are oval shaped; spiral, which have arms spiraling outward from a central bulge; and irregular, which have no obvious shape. Sometimes, the shape of a galaxy is distorted by a collision with another galaxy. Quasars (quasi-stellar objects) are thought to be galactic nuclei but are so far away that their exact nature is still uncertain. They are compact, highly luminous objects in the outer reaches of the known Universe; while the farthest known "ordinary" galaxies are about 10 billion light-years away, the farthest known quasar is about 15 billion light-years away. Active galaxies, such as Seyfert galaxies and radio galaxies, emit intense radiation. In a Seyfert galaxy, this radiation comes from the galactic nucleus; in a radio galaxy, it also comes from huge lobes on either side of the galaxy. The radiation from active galaxies and quasars is thought to be caused by black holes (see pp. 24-25).

OPTICAL IMAGE OF NGC 4486 (ELLIPTICAL GALAXY)

Globular cluster containing very old red giants

Central region containing old red giants

Less densely populated region

Neighboring galaxy

OPTICAL IMAGE OF LARGE MAGELLANIC CLOUD (IRREGULAR GALAXY)

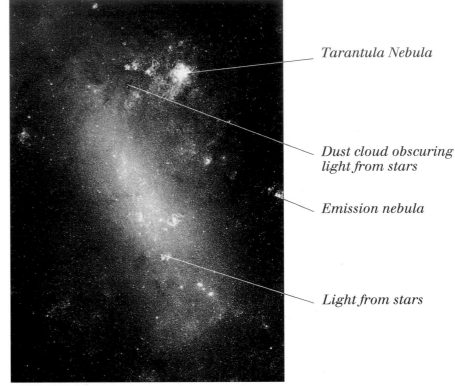

Tarantula Nebula

Dust cloud obscuring light from stars

Emission nebula

Light from stars

OPTICAL IMAGE OF NGC 2997 (SPIRAL GALAXY)

Glowing nebula in spiral arm

Spiral arm containing young stars

Galactic nucleus containing old stars

Dust in spiral arm reflecting blue light from hot young stars

Hot, ionized hydrogen gas emitting red light

Dust lane

OPTICAL IMAGE OF CENTAURUS A (RADIO GALAXY)

Dust lane crossing elliptical galaxy

Galactic nucleus containing powerful source of radiation

Light from old stars

COLOR-ENHANCED RADIO IMAGE OF CENTAURUS A

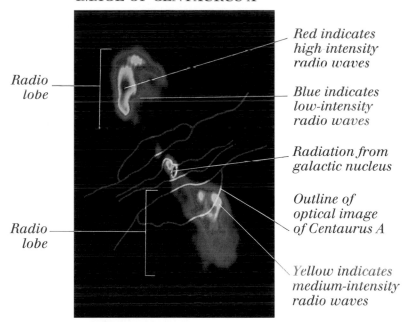

Radio lobe

Radio lobe

Red indicates high intensity radio waves

Blue indicates low-intensity radio waves

Radiation from galactic nucleus

Outline of optical image of Centaurus A

Yellow indicates medium-intensity radio waves

COLOR-ENHANCED RADIO IMAGE OF 3C273 (QUASAR)

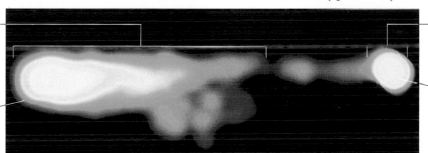

Radiation from jet of high-energy particles moving away from quasar

Blue indicates low-intensity radio waves

Quasar nucleus

White indicates high-intensity radio waves

OPTICAL IMAGE OF NGC 1566 (SEYFERT GALAXY)

Nebula in spiral arm

Compact nucleus emitting intense radiation

Spiral arm

COLOR-ENHANCED OPTICAL IMAGE OF NGC 5754 (TWO COLLIDING GALAXIES)

Blue indicates low-intensity radiation

Red indicates medium-intensity radiation

Spiral arm distorted by gravitational influence of smaller galaxy

Large spiral galaxy

Smaller galaxy colliding with larger galaxy

Yellow indicates high-intensity radiation

9

The Milky Way

VIEW TOWARD GALACTIC CENTER

THE MILKY WAY IS THE NAME GIVEN TO THE FAINT BAND OF LIGHT that stretches across the night sky. This light comes from stars and nebulae in our galaxy, known as the Milky Way Galaxy or simply as "the Galaxy." The Galaxy is shaped like a spiral, with a dense central bulge that is encircled by four arms spiraling outward and surrounded by a less dense halo. We cannot see the spiral shape because our Solar System is in one of the spiral arms, the Orion Arm (also called the Local Arm). From our position, the center of the Galaxy is completely obscured by dust clouds; as a result, optical maps give only a limited view of the Galaxy. However, a more complete picture can be obtained by studying radio, infrared, and other radiation. The central bulge of the Galaxy is a relatively small, dense sphere that contains mainly older red and yellow stars. The halo is a less dense region in which the oldest stars are situated; some of these stars may be as old as the Galaxy itself (possibly 15 billion years). The spiral arms contain mainly hot, young, blue stars, as well as nebulae (clouds of dust and gas, inside which stars are born). The Galaxy is vast—about 100,000 light-years across (a light-year is about 5,879 billion miles); in comparison, the Solar System seems small, at about 12 light-hours across (about 8 billion miles). The entire Galaxy is rotating in space, although the inner stars travel faster than those further out. The Sun, which is about two-thirds out from the center, completes one lap of the Galaxy about every 220 million years.

PANORAMIC OPTICAL MAP OF OUR GALAXY AND NEARBY GALAXIES

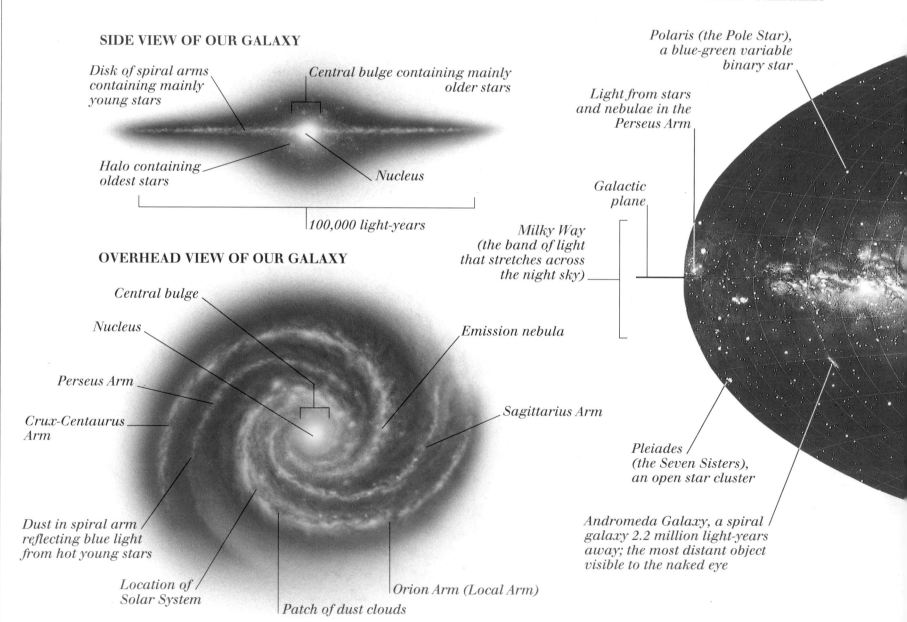

SIDE VIEW OF OUR GALAXY

Disk of spiral arms containing mainly young stars

Central bulge containing mainly older stars

Halo containing oldest stars

Nucleus

100,000 light-years

OVERHEAD VIEW OF OUR GALAXY

Central bulge

Nucleus

Perseus Arm

Crux-Centaurus Arm

Emission nebula

Sagittarius Arm

Dust in spiral arm reflecting blue light from hot young stars

Location of Solar System

Patch of dust clouds

Orion Arm (Local Arm)

Polaris (the Pole Star), a blue-green variable binary star

Light from stars and nebulae in the Perseus Arm

Galactic plane

Milky Way (the band of light that stretches across the night sky)

Pleiades (the Seven Sisters), an open star cluster

Andromeda Galaxy, a spiral galaxy 2.2 million light-years away; the most distant object visible to the naked eye

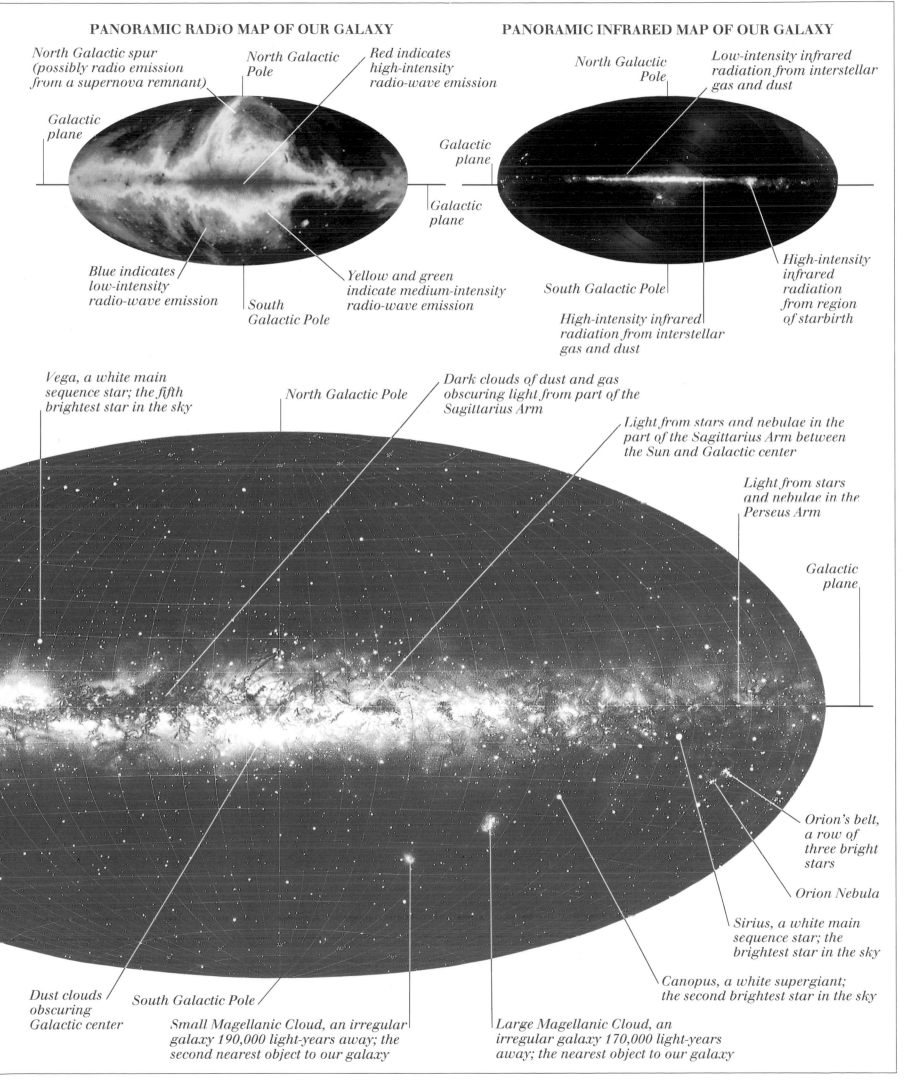

PANORAMIC RADIO MAP OF OUR GALAXY

North Galactic spur (possibly radio emission from a supernova remnant)

North Galactic Pole

Red indicates high-intensity radio-wave emission

Galactic plane

Blue indicates low-intensity radio-wave emission

South Galactic Pole

Yellow and green indicate medium-intensity radio-wave emission

PANORAMIC INFRARED MAP OF OUR GALAXY

North Galactic Pole

Low-intensity infrared radiation from interstellar gas and dust

Galactic plane

Galactic plane

South Galactic Pole

High-intensity infrared radiation from interstellar gas and dust

High-intensity infrared radiation from region of starbirth

Vega, a white main sequence star; the fifth brightest star in the sky

North Galactic Pole

Dark clouds of dust and gas obscuring light from part of the Sagittarius Arm

Light from stars and nebulae in the part of the Sagittarius Arm between the Sun and Galactic center

Light from stars and nebulae in the Perseus Arm

Galactic plane

Orion's belt, a row of three bright stars

Orion Nebula

Sirius, a white main sequence star; the brightest star in the sky

Canopus, a white supergiant; the second brightest star in the sky

Dust clouds obscuring Galactic center

South Galactic Pole

Small Magellanic Cloud, an irregular galaxy 190,000 light-years away; the second nearest object to our galaxy

Large Magellanic Cloud, an irregular galaxy 170,000 light-years away; the nearest object to our galaxy

11

Nebulae and star clusters

**HODGE 11, A
GLOBULAR CLUSTER**

A NEBULA IS A CLOUD OF DUST AND GAS inside a galaxy. Nebulae become visible if the gas glows or if the cloud reflects starlight or obscures light from more distant objects. Emission nebulae shine because their gas emits light when it is stimulated by radiation from hot young stars. Reflection nebulae shine because their dust reflects light from stars in or around the nebula. Dark nebulae appear as silhouettes because they block light from shining nebulae or stars behind them. Two types of nebula are associated with dying stars: planetary nebulae and supernova remnants. Both consist of expanding shells of gas that were once the outer layers of a star. A planetary nebula is a gas shell drifting away from a dying stellar core. A supernova remnant is a gas shell moving away from a stellar core at great speed following a violent explosion called a supernova (see pp. 22-23). Stars are often found in groups known as clusters. Open clusters are loose groups of a few thousand young stars that were born in the same cloud and are drifting apart. Globular clusters are densely packed, roughly spherical groups of hundreds of thousands of older stars.

TRIFFID NEBULA (EMISSION NEBULA)

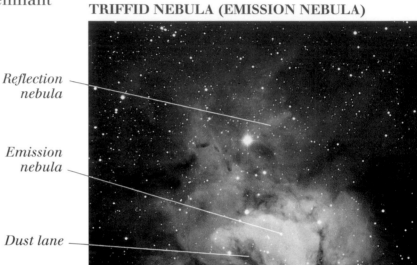

Reflection nebula

Emission nebula

Dust lane

Starbirth region (area in which dust and gas combine to form stars)

**PLEIADES (OPEN STAR CLUSTER)
WITH A REFLECTION NEBULA**

Wisps of dust and hydrogen gas remaining from cloud in which stars formed

Young star in an open cluster of 300–500 stars

Reflection nebula

HORSEHEAD NEBULA (DARK NEBULA)

Glowing filament of hot, ionized hydrogen gas

Alnitak (star in Orion's belt)

Dust lane

Emission nebula

Star near southern end of Orion's belt

Emission nebula

Horsehead Nebula

Reflection nebula

Dark nebula obscuring light from distant stars

ORION NEBULA (DIFFUSE EMISSION NEBULA)

Glowing cloud of dust and hydrogen gas forming part of Orion Nebula

Dust cloud

Trapezium (group of four young stars)

Red light from hot, ionized hydrogen gas

Gas cloud emitting light because of ultraviolet radiation from the four young Trapezium stars

Green light from hot, ionized oxygen gas

Glowing filament of hot, ionized hydrogen gas

HELIX NEBULA (PLANETARY NEBULA)

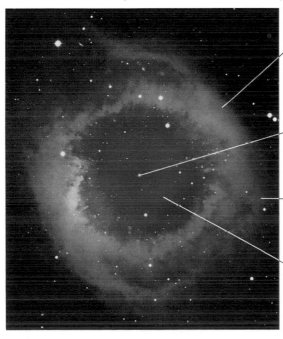

Planetary nebula (gas shell expanding outward from dying stellar core)

Stellar core at a temperature of about 180,000°F

Red light from hot, ionized hydrogen gas

Blue-green light from hot, ionized oxygen and nitrogen gases

VELA SUPERNOVA REMNANT

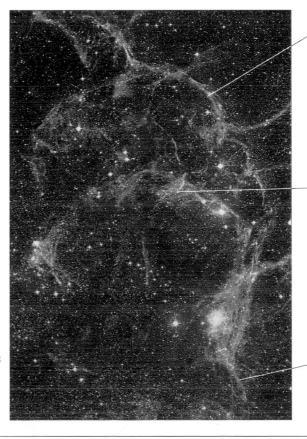

Supernova remnant (gas shell consisting of outer layers of star thrown off in supernova explosion)

Hydrogen gas emitting red light due to being heated by supernova explosion

Glowing filament of hot, ionized hydrogen gas

Stars of northern skies

WHEN YOU LOOK AT THE NORTHERN SKY, you look away from the densely populated Galactic center, so the northern sky generally appears less bright than the southern sky (see pp. 16-17). Among the best-known sights in the northern sky are the constellations Ursa Major (the Great Bear) and Orion. Some ancient civilizations believed that the stars were fixed to a celestial sphere surrounding the Earth, and modern maps of the sky are based on a similar idea. The North and South Poles of this imaginary celestial sphere are directly above the North and South Poles of the Earth, at the points where the Earth's axis of rotation intersects the sphere. The celestial North Pole is at the center of the map shown here, and Polaris (the Pole Star) lies very close to it. The celestial equator marks a projection of the Earth's equator on the sphere. The ecliptic marks the path of the Sun across the sky as the Earth orbits the Sun. The Moon and planets move against the background of the stars because the stars are much more distant; the nearest star outside the Solar System (Proxima Centauri) is more than 50,000 times farther away than the planet Jupiter.

ORION

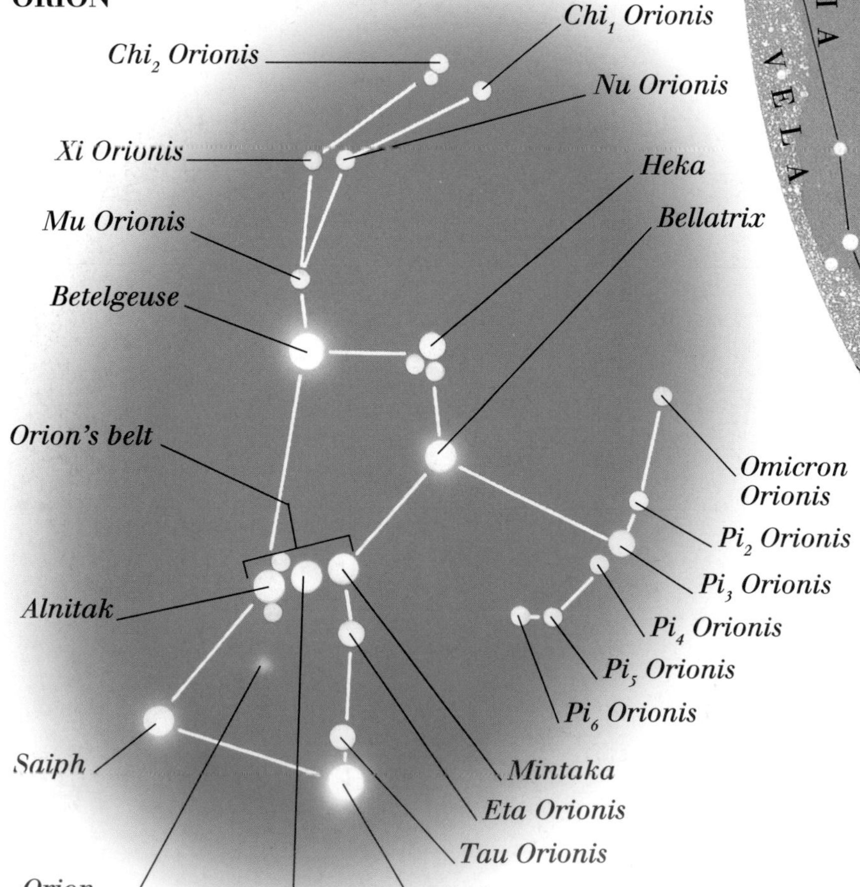

Chi₁ Orionis — $Chi_1\ Orionis$
Chi₂ Orionis
Nu Orionis
Xi Orionis
Heka
Mu Orionis
Bellatrix
Betelgeuse
Orion's belt
Omicron Orionis
Pi₂ Orionis
Pi₃ Orionis
Pi₄ Orionis
Alnitak
Pi₅ Orionis
Pi₆ Orionis
Saiph
Mintaka
Eta Orionis
Tau Orionis
Orion Nebula
Rigel
Alnilam

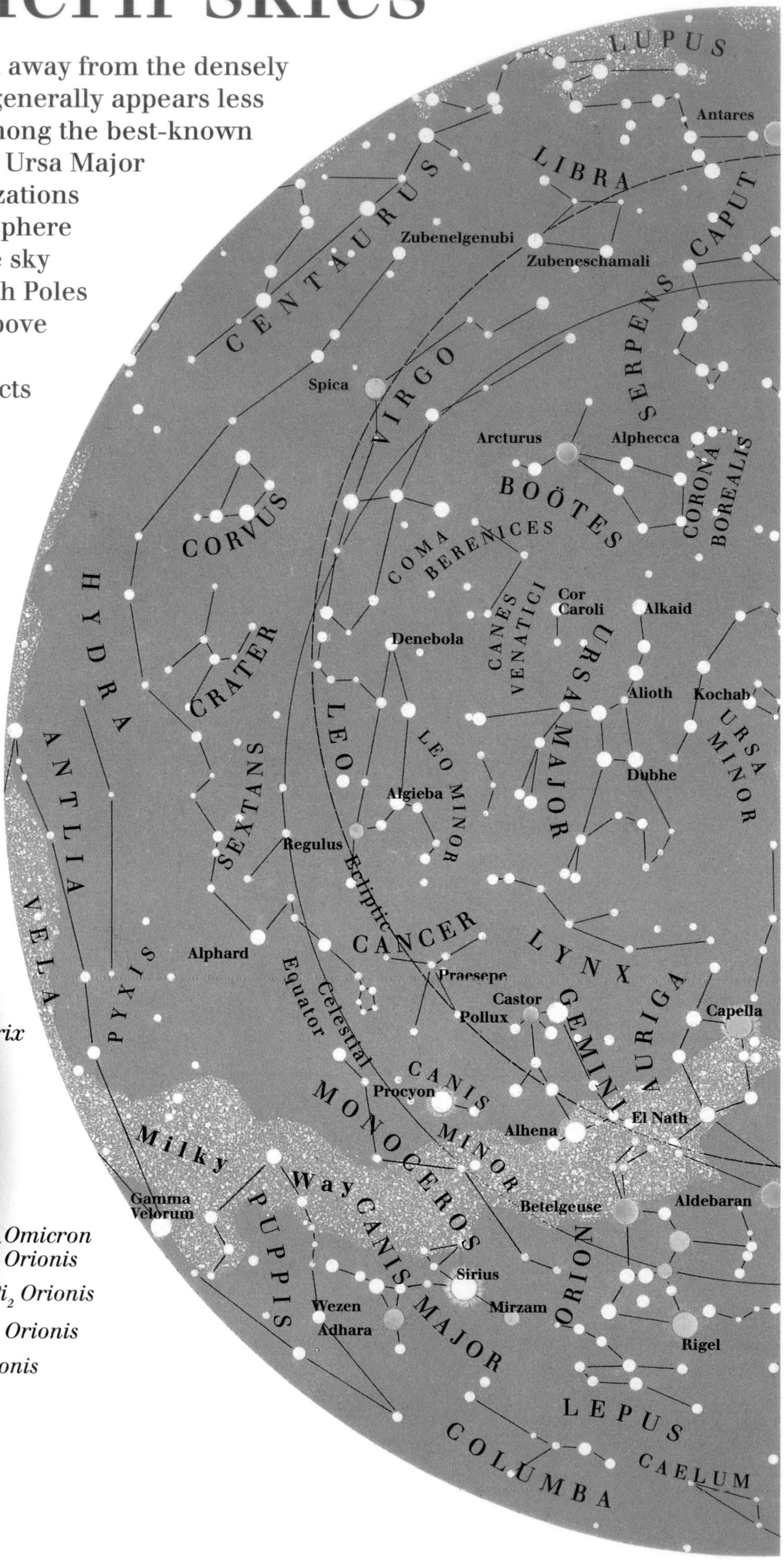

VISIBLE STARS IN THE NORTHERN SKY

14

THE PLOW, PART OF URSA MAJOR (THE GREAT BEAR)

Alcor

Alkaid

Dubhe

Mizar

Alioth

Megrez

Phekda

Merak

SCORPIUS

Shaula

CORONA AUSTRALIS

Kaus Australis

Nunki

OPHIUCHUS

SERPENS CAUDA

SCUTUM

SAGITTARIUS

AQUILA

CAPRICORNUS

HERCULES

Ras Alhague

Ecliptic

LYRA

Vega

Altair

DRACO

Eltanin

CYGNUS

VULPECULA

DELPHINUS

Deneb

Enif

EQUULEUS

AQUARIUS

Deneb Algedi

Al Nair

CEPHEUS

Alderamin

LACERTA

PEGASUS

PISCES AUSTRINUS

GRUS

Polaris

CASSIOPEIA

Schedar

Scheat

Markab

Fomalhaut

Alpheratz

ANDROMEDA

Algenib

SCULPTOR

Mirach

Mirfak

Almach

PISCES

PERSEUS

Algol

TRIANGULUM

Hamal

ARIES

Pleiades

Celestial Equator

Deneb Kaitos

Nair Al Zaurak

PHOENIX

TAURUS

Mira

Menkar

CETUS

ERIDANUS

FORNAX

Acamar

PEGASUS AND ANDROMEDA

Theta Pegasi

Enif

Lambda Pegasi

Kappa Pegasi

Hamal

Pi Pegasi

Iota Pegasi

Xi Pegasi

Mu Pegasi

Matar

Scheat

Markab

Omicron Andromedae

Lambda Andromedae

Algenib

Theta Andromedae

Andromeda Galaxy

Alpheratz

Nu Andromedae

Phi Andromedae

Delta Andromedae

51 Andromedae

Mirach

Mu Andromedae

Almach

15

Stars of southern skies

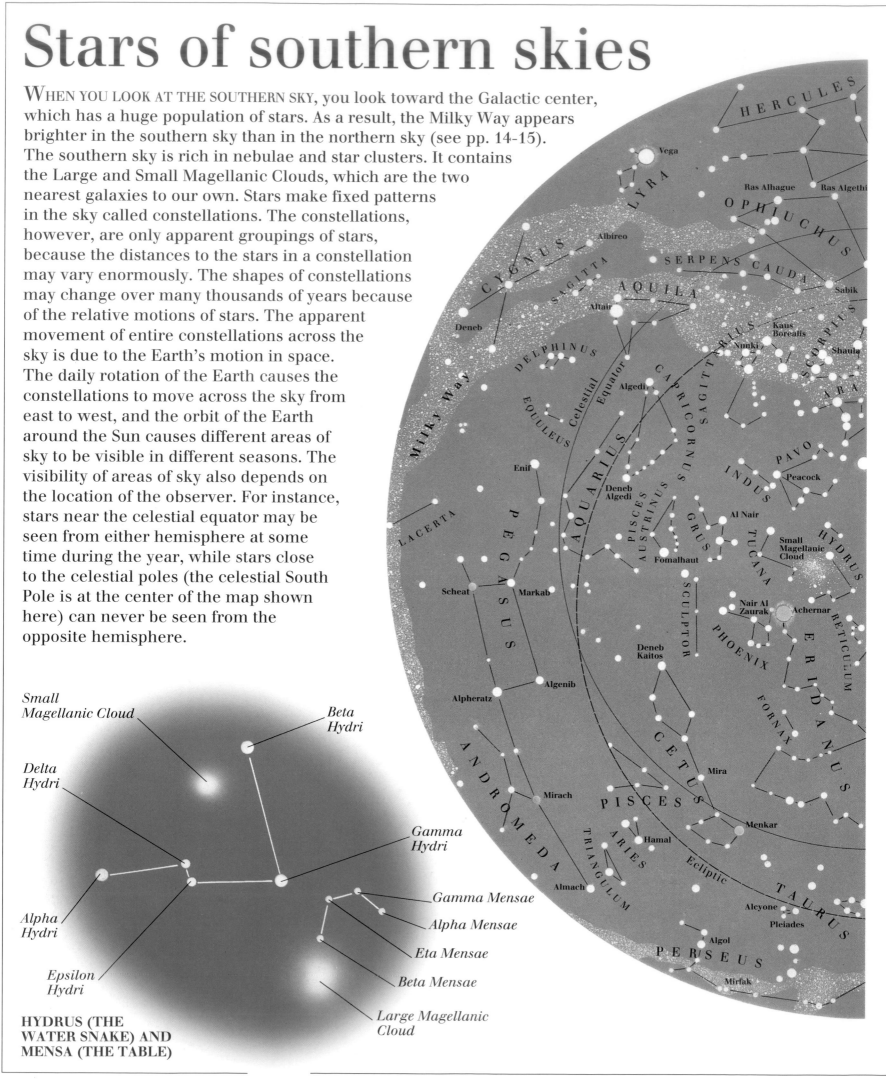

WHEN YOU LOOK AT THE SOUTHERN SKY, you look toward the Galactic center, which has a huge population of stars. As a result, the Milky Way appears brighter in the southern sky than in the northern sky (see pp. 14-15). The southern sky is rich in nebulae and star clusters. It contains the Large and Small Magellanic Clouds, which are the two nearest galaxies to our own. Stars make fixed patterns in the sky called constellations. The constellations, however, are only apparent groupings of stars, because the distances to the stars in a constellation may vary enormously. The shapes of constellations may change over many thousands of years because of the relative motions of stars. The apparent movement of entire constellations across the sky is due to the Earth's motion in space. The daily rotation of the Earth causes the constellations to move across the sky from east to west, and the orbit of the Earth around the Sun causes different areas of sky to be visible in different seasons. The visibility of areas of sky also depends on the location of the observer. For instance, stars near the celestial equator may be seen from either hemisphere at some time during the year, while stars close to the celestial poles (the celestial South Pole is at the center of the map shown here) can never be seen from the opposite hemisphere.

Small Magellanic Cloud

Delta Hydri

Alpha Hydri

Epsilon Hydri

Beta Hydri

Gamma Hydri

Gamma Mensae

Alpha Mensae

Eta Mensae

Beta Mensae

Large Magellanic Cloud

HYDRUS (THE WATER SNAKE) AND MENSA (THE TABLE)

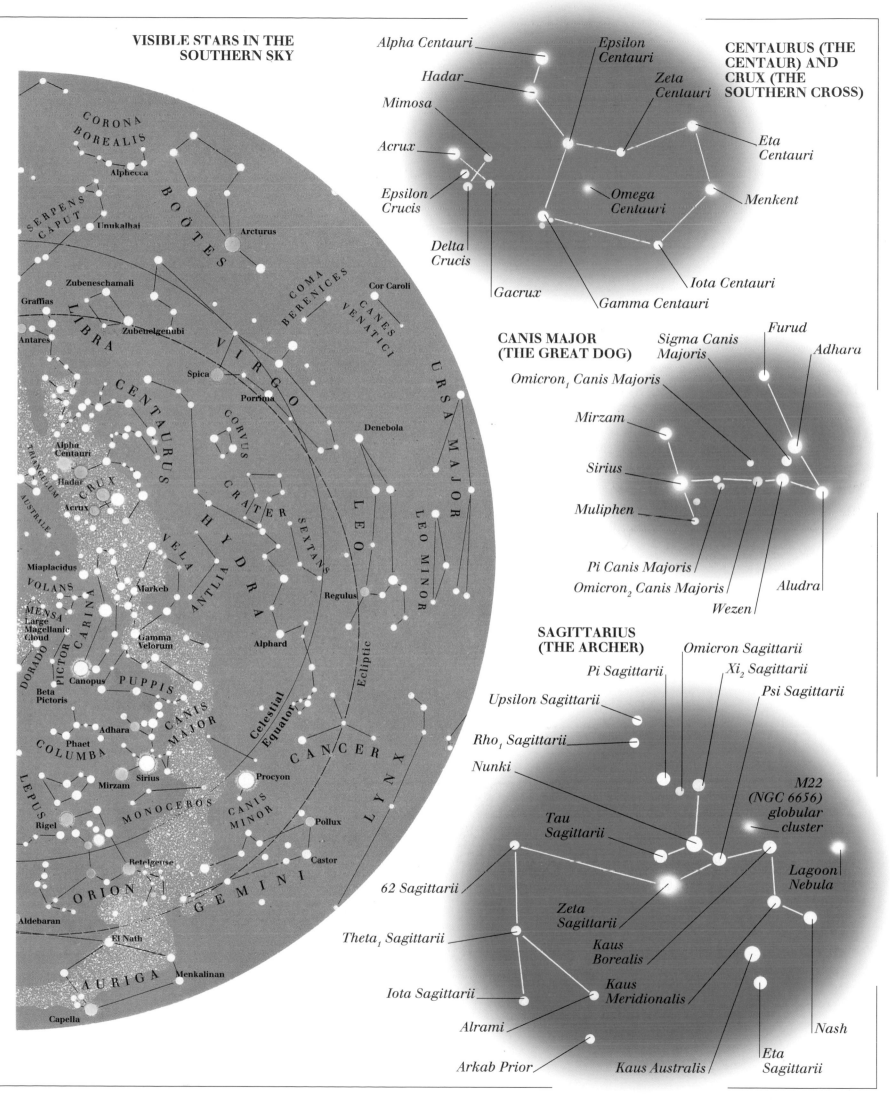

VISIBLE STARS IN THE SOUTHERN SKY

CORONA BOREALIS
Alphecca
SERPENS CAPUT
Unukalhai
BOÖTES
Arcturus
COMA BERENICES
Cor Caroli
CANES VENATICI
Zubeneschamali
Graffias
LIBRA
Antares
Zubenelgenubi
VIRGO
URSA MAJOR
Spica
Porrima
Denebola
CENTAURUS
CORVUS
CRATER
SEXTANS
LEO
LEO MINOR
Alpha Centauri
HYDRA
Hadar
CRUX
Acrux
VELA
Miaplacidus
VOLANS
Markeb
ANTLIA
Regulus
MENSA
Large Magellanic Cloud
CARINA
PICTOR
Gamma Velorum
Alphard
DORADO
Canopus
PUPPIS
Ecliptic
Celestial Equator
CANCER
Beta Pictoris
Adhara
CANIS MAJOR
Phaet
COLUMBA
Mirzam
Sirius
Procyon
CANIS MINOR
Pollux
LYNX
LEPUS
Rigel
MONOCEROS
Castor
GEMINI
Betelgeuse
ORION
Aldebaran
El Nath
AURIGA
Menkalinan
Capella
TRIANGULUM AUSTRALE

CENTAURUS (THE CENTAUR) AND CRUX (THE SOUTHERN CROSS)

Alpha Centauri
Epsilon Centauri
Hadar
Zeta Centauri
Mimosa
Acrux
Eta Centauri
Epsilon Crucis
Omega Centauri
Menkent
Delta Crucis
Gacrux
Gamma Centauri
Iota Centauri

CANIS MAJOR (THE GREAT DOG)

Sigma Canis Majoris
Furud
Adhara
Omicron₁ Canis Majoris
Mirzam
Sirius
Muliphen
Pi Canis Majoris
Omicron₂ Canis Majoris
Aludra
Wezen

SAGITTARIUS (THE ARCHER)

Omicron Sagittarii
Pi Sagittarii
Xi₂ Sagittarii
Upsilon Sagittarii
Psi Sagittarii
Rho₁ Sagittarii
Nunki
M22 (NGC 6656) globular cluster
Tau Sagittarii
62 Sagittarii
Zeta Sagittarii
Lagoon Nebula
Theta₁ Sagittarii
Kaus Borealis
Iota Sagittarii
Kaus Meridionalis
Alrami
Nash
Arkab Prior
Kaus Australis
Eta Sagittarii

Stars

OPEN STAR CLUSTER AND DUST CLOUD

STARS ARE BODIES of hot glowing gas that are born in nebulae (see pp. 20-23). They vary enormously in size, mass, and temperature: diameters range from about 450 times smaller to over 1,000 times bigger than that of the Sun; masses range from about a twentieth to over 50 solar masses; and surface temperatures range from about 5,500°F to over 90,000°F. The color of a star is determined by its temperature: the hottest stars are blue and the coolest are red. The Sun, with a surface temperature of 10,000°F, is between these extremes and appears yellow. The energy emitted by a shining star is produced by nuclear fusion in the star's core. The brightness of a star is measured in magnitudes—the brighter the star, the lower its magnitude. There are two types of magnitude: apparent magnitude, which is the brightness seen from Earth, and absolute magnitude, which is the brightness that would be seen from a standard distance of 10 parsecs (32.6 light-years). The light emitted by a star may be split to form a spectrum containing a series of dark lines (absorption lines). The patterns of lines indicate the presence of particular chemical elements, enabling astronomers to deduce the composition of the star's atmosphere. The magnitude and spectral type (color) of stars may be plotted on a graph called a Hertzsprung-Russell diagram, which shows that stars tend to fall into several well-defined groups. The principal groups are main sequence stars (those which are fusing hydrogen to form helium), giants, supergiants, and white dwarfs.

STAR SIZES

Red giant (diameters between about 10 million and 100 million miles)

The Sun (main sequence star with diameter about 870,000 miles)

White dwarf (diameters between about 2,000 and 30,000 miles)

ENERGY EMISSION FROM THE SUN

Nuclear fusion in core produces gamma rays and neutrinos

Neutrinos travel to Earth directly from Sun's core in about 8 minutes

Lower-energy radiation travels to Earth in about 8 minutes

Earth

Lower-energy radiation (mainly ultraviolet, infrared, and light rays) leaves surface

Sun

High-energy radiation (gamma rays) loses energy while traveling to surface over 2 million years

STAR MAGNITUDES

APPARENT MAGNITUDE

Brighter stars

-9

0

+9

Fainter stars

Sirius: apparent magnitude of -1.46

Rigel: apparent magnitude of +0.12

Objects of magnitude higher than about +5.5 cannot be seen by the naked eye

ABSOLUTE MAGNITUDE

Rigel: absolute magnitude of -7.1

Sirius: absolute magnitude of +1.4

NUCLEAR FUSION IN MAIN SEQUENCE STARS LIKE THE SUN

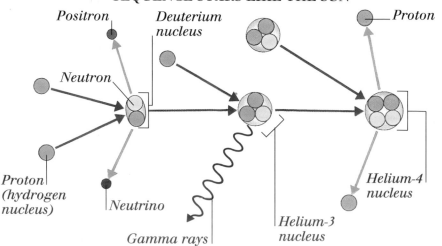

Positron

Deuterium nucleus

Proton

Neutron

Proton (hydrogen nucleus)

Neutrino

Gamma rays

Helium-3 nucleus

Helium-4 nucleus

HERTZSPRUNG-RUSSELL DIAGRAM

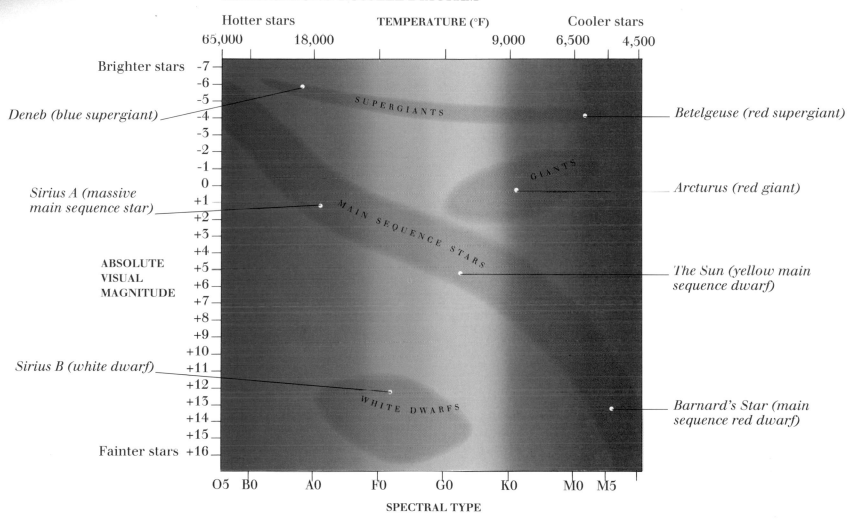

Hotter stars TEMPERATURE (°F) Cooler stars

65,000   18,000   9,000   6,500   4,500

Brighter stars   -7
    -6
    -5
Deneb (blue supergiant)   -4   SUPERGIANTS   Betelgeuse (red supergiant)
    -3
    -2
    -1
    0   GIANTS   Arcturus (red giant)
Sirius A (massive   +1
main sequence star)   +2   MAIN SEQUENCE STARS
    +3
    +4
ABSOLUTE   +5   The Sun (yellow main
VISUAL   +6   sequence dwarf)
MAGNITUDE   +7
    +8
    +9
    +10
Sirius B (white dwarf)   +11
    +12
    +13   WHITE DWARFS   Barnard's Star (main
    +14   sequence red dwarf)
    +15
Fainter stars   +16

O5   B0   A0   F0   G0   K0   M0   M5

SPECTRAL TYPE

STELLAR SPECTRAL ABSORPTION LINES

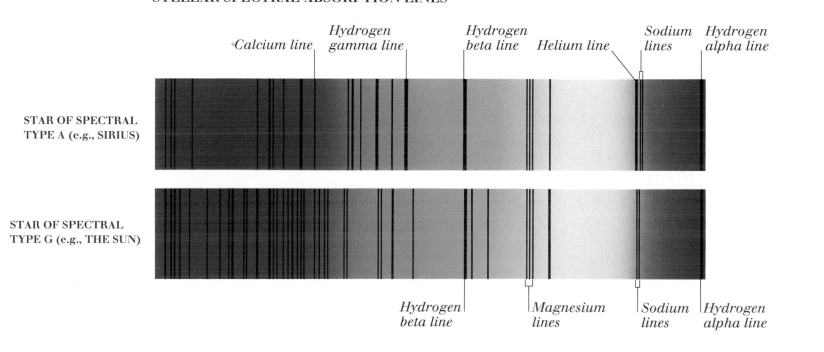

Calcium line   Hydrogen gamma line   Hydrogen beta line   Helium line   Sodium lines   Hydrogen alpha line

STAR OF SPECTRAL
TYPE A (e.g., SIRIUS)

STAR OF SPECTRAL
TYPE G (e.g., THE SUN)

Hydrogen beta line   Magnesium lines   Sodium lines   Hydrogen alpha line

Small stars

SMALL STARS HAVE A MASS of up to about one and a half times that of the Sun. They begin to form when a region of higher density in a nebula condenses into a huge globule of gas and dust that contracts under its own gravity. Within a globule, regions of condensing matter heat up and begin to glow, forming protostars. If a protostar contains enough matter, the central temperature reaches about 27 million °F. At this temperature, nuclear reactions in which hydrogen fuses to form helium can start. This process releases energy, which prevents the star from contracting further, and also causes it to shine; it is now a main sequence star. A star of about one solar mass remains in the main sequence for about 10 billion years, until the hydrogen in the star's core has been converted into helium. The helium core then contracts again, and nuclear reactions continue in a shell around the core. The core becomes hot enough for helium to fuse to form carbon, while the outer layers of the star expand, cool, and shine less brightly. The expanding star is known as a red giant. When the helium in the core runs out, the outer layers of the star may drift off as an expanding gas shell called a planetary nebula. The remaining core (about 80 percent of the original star) is now in its final stages. It becomes a white dwarf star that gradually cools and dims. When it finally stops shining altogether, the dead star will become a black dwarf.

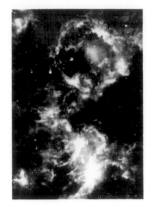

REGION OF STAR FORMATION IN ORION

STRUCTURE OF A MAIN SEQUENCE STAR

Core containing hydrogen fusing to form helium

Radiative zone

Convective zone

Surface temperature about 10,000°F

Core temperature about 27 million °F

STRUCTURE OF A NEBULA

Young main sequence star

Dense region of dust and gas (mainly hydrogen) condensing under gravity to form globules

Hot, ionized hydrogen gas emitting red light due to stimulation by radiation from hot young stars

Dark globule of dust and gas (mainly hydrogen) contracting to form protostars

LIFE OF A SMALL STAR OF ABOUT ONE SOLAR MASS

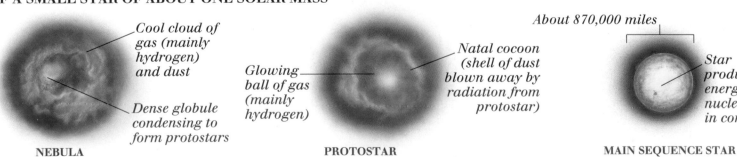

Cool cloud of gas (mainly hydrogen) and dust

Dense globule condensing to form protostars

NEBULA

Glowing ball of gas (mainly hydrogen)

Natal cocoon (shell of dust blown away by radiation from protostar)

PROTOSTAR
Duration: 50 million years

About 870,000 miles

Star producing energy by nuclear fusion in core

MAIN SEQUENCE STAR
Duration: 10 billion years

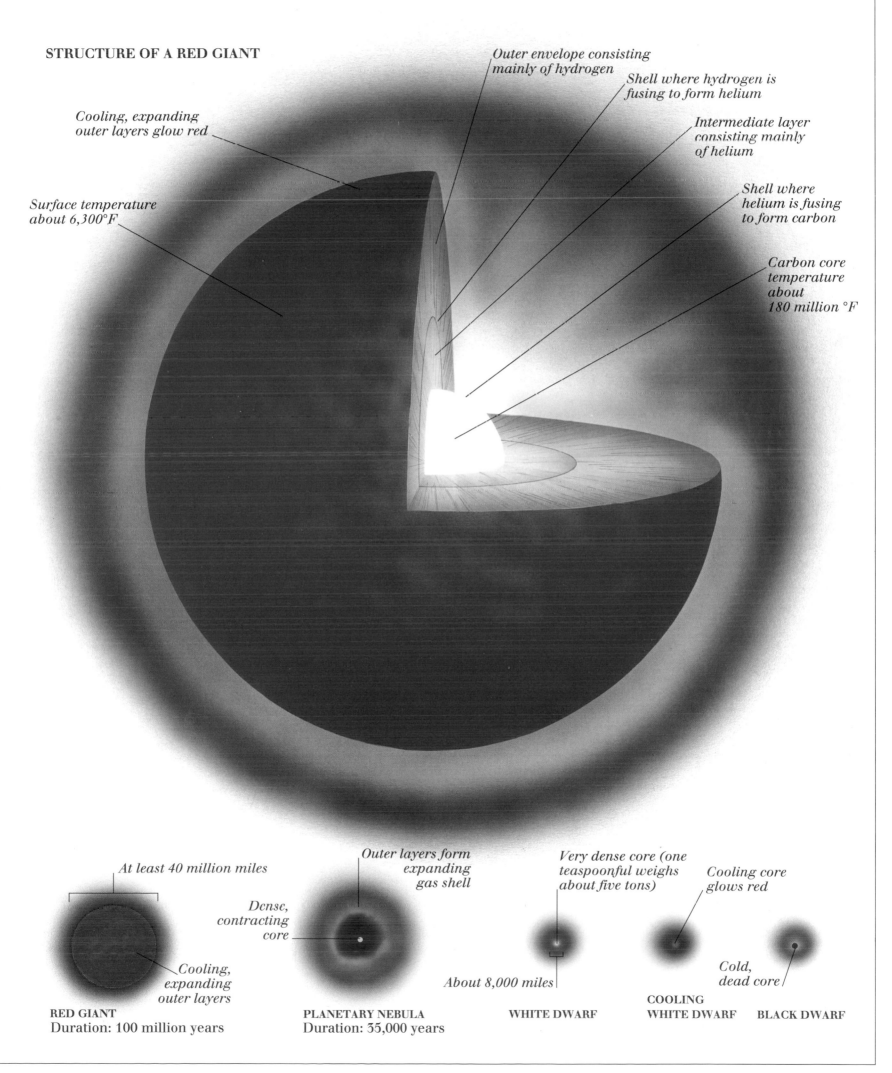

STRUCTURE OF A RED GIANT

Cooling, expanding outer layers glow red

Surface temperature about 6,300°F

Outer envelope consisting mainly of hydrogen

Shell where hydrogen is fusing to form helium

Intermediate layer consisting mainly of helium

Shell where helium is fusing to form carbon

Carbon core temperature about 180 million °F

At least 40 million miles

Cooling, expanding outer layers

RED GIANT
Duration: 100 million years

Outer layers form expanding gas shell

Dense, contracting core

PLANETARY NEBULA
Duration: 35,000 years

Very dense core (one teaspoonful weighs about five tons)

About 8,000 miles

WHITE DWARF

Cooling core glows red

Cold, dead core

COOLING WHITE DWARF

BLACK DWARF

Massive stars

MASSIVE STARS HAVE A MASS AT LEAST THREE TIMES that of the Sun, and some
stars are as massive as about 50 Suns. A massive star evolves in a similar way to
a small star until it reaches the main sequence stage (see pp. 20-21). During the
main sequence, a star shines steadily until the hydrogen in its core has fused to
form helium. This process takes billions of years in a small star, but only millions
of years in a massive star. A massive star then becomes a red supergiant, which
initially consists of a helium core surrounded by outer layers of cooling, expanding
gas. Over the next few million years, a series of nuclear reactions form different
elements in shells around an iron core. The core eventually collapses in less than
a second, causing a massive explosion called
a supernova, in which a shock wave blows
away the outer layers of the star.
Supernovae shine brighter than
an entire galaxy for a short
time. Sometimes, the core
survives the supernova
explosion. If the surviving
core is between about
one and a half and
three solar masses, it
contracts to become
a tiny, dense neutron
star. If the core is
considerably greater
than three solar
masses, it contracts
to become a black
hole (see pp. 24-25).

SUPERNOVA

**TARANTULA NEBULA BEFORE
SUPERNOVA**

**STRUCTURE
OF A RED SUPERGIANT**

*Outer envelope consisting
mainly of hydrogen*

*Layer consisting
mainly of helium*

*Layer consisting
mainly of carbon*

*Layer consisting
mainly of oxygen*

*Layer consisting
mainly of silicon*

*Shell of hydrogen
fusing to form
helium*

*Shell of helium
fusing to form
carbon*

*Shell of carbon
fusing to form
oxygen*

*Shell of oxygen fusing
to form silicon*

*Shell of silicon fusing
to form iron core*

*Surface temperature
about 5,500°F*

*Cooling, expanding
outer layers glow red*

*Core of mainly iron at a
temperature of 5.4–9 billion °F*

**LIFE OF A MASSIVE STAR OF
ABOUT 10 SOLAR MASSES**

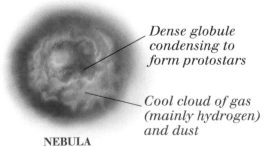

*Dense globule
condensing to
form protostars*

*Cool cloud of gas
(mainly hydrogen)
and dust*

NEBULA

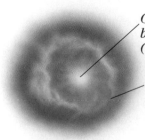

*Glowing
ball of gas
(mainly hydrogen)*

*Natal cocoon (shell
of dust blown away
by radiation from
protostar)*

PROTOSTAR
Duration: a few hundred
thousand years

*About
2 million miles*

*Star producing
energy by nuclear
fusion in
core*

MAIN SEQUENCE STAR
Duration: 10 million years

FEATURES OF A SUPERNOVA

TARANTULA NEBULA SHOWING SUPERNOVA IN 1987

Ejecta (outer layers of star thrown off during explosion) travels at speeds of up to 6,000 miles/sec

Shock wave travels outward from core at speeds of up to 20,000 miles/sec

Reverse shock wave moves inward and heats ejecta, causing it to shine

Heavy chemical elements are scattered through space by explosion

Central temperature more than 18 billion °F

Contracting core consisting mainly of neutrons remains after explosion

Light energy of a billion Suns emitted during explosion

Extremely dense core (one teaspoonful weighs about a billion tons)

About 6 miles

Core mass of less than three solar masses

NEUTRON STAR

About 60 million miles

Outer layers of star blown off in explosion

Contracting stellar core may remain after supernova

Core of mass greater than three solar masses continues contracting to become black hole

Cooling, expanding outer layers

Accretion disk

RED SUPERGIANT
Duration: 4 million years

SUPERNOVA
Duration of visibility: 1–2 years

BLACK HOLE

23

Neutron stars and black holes

NEUTRON STARS AND BLACK HOLES form from the stellar cores that remain after stars have exploded as supernovae (see pp. 22-23). If the remaining core is between about one and a half and three solar masses, it contracts to form a neutron star. If the remaining core is considerably greater than about three solar masses, it contracts to form a black hole. Neutron stars are typically only about six miles in diameter and consist almost entirely of subatomic particles called neutrons. These stars are so dense that a teaspoonful would weigh about a billion tons. Neutron stars are observed as pulsars, so-called because they rotate rapidly and emit two beams of radio waves, which sweep across the sky and are detected as short pulses. Black holes are characterized by their extremely strong gravity, which is so powerful that not even light can escape; as a result, black holes are invisible. However, they may be detected if they have a close companion star. The gravity of the black hole pulls gas from the other star, forming an accretion disk that spirals around the black hole at high speed, heating up and emitting radiation. Eventually, the matter spirals in to cross the event horizon (the boundary of the black hole), finally disappearing from the visible Universe.

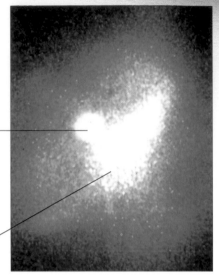

X-ray emission from pulsar (neutron star rotating 30 times each second)

X-ray emission from center of nebula

X-RAY IMAGE OF THE CRAB NEBULA (SUPERNOVA REMNANT)

PULSAR (ROTATING NEUTRON STAR)

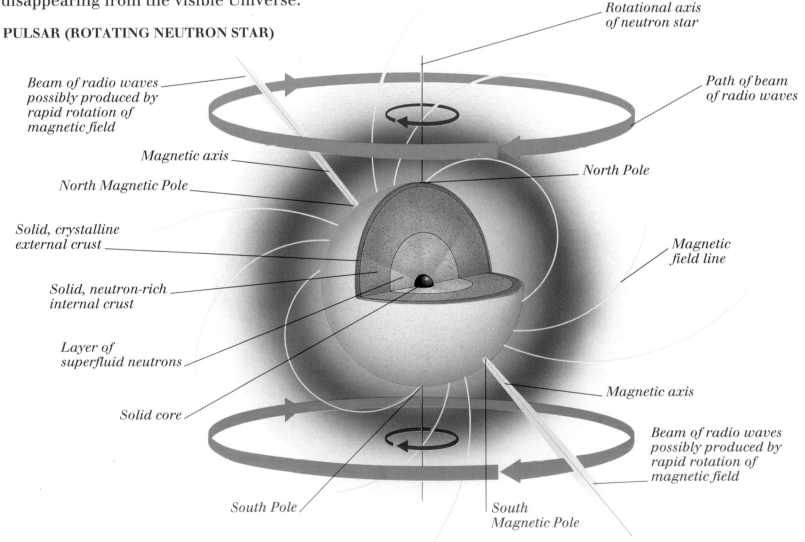

Rotational axis of neutron star

Beam of radio waves possibly produced by rapid rotation of magnetic field

Path of beam of radio waves

Magnetic axis

North Pole

North Magnetic Pole

Solid, crystalline external crust

Magnetic field line

Solid, neutron-rich internal crust

Layer of superfluid neutrons

Magnetic axis

Solid core

Beam of radio waves possibly produced by rapid rotation of magnetic field

South Pole

South Magnetic Pole

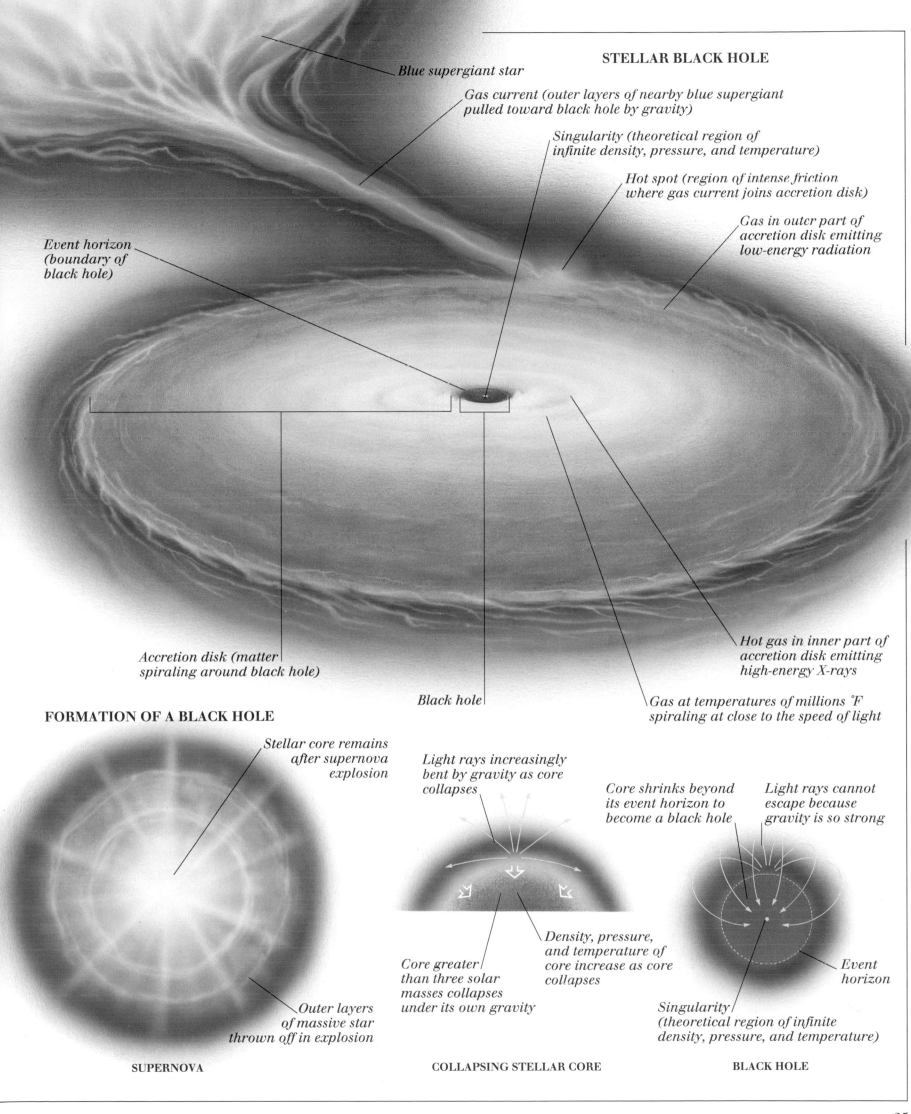

STELLAR BLACK HOLE

Blue supergiant star

Gas current (outer layers of nearby blue supergiant pulled toward black hole by gravity)

Singularity (theoretical region of infinite density, pressure, and temperature)

Hot spot (region of intense friction where gas current joins accretion disk)

Gas in outer part of accretion disk emitting low-energy radiation

Event horizon (boundary of black hole)

Accretion disk (matter spiraling around black hole)

Black hole

Hot gas in inner part of accretion disk emitting high-energy X-rays

Gas at temperatures of millions °F spiraling at close to the speed of light

FORMATION OF A BLACK HOLE

Stellar core remains after supernova explosion

Light rays increasingly bent by gravity as core collapses

Core shrinks beyond its event horizon to become a black hole

Light rays cannot escape because gravity is so strong

Density, pressure, and temperature of core increase as core collapses

Outer layers of massive star thrown off in explosion

Core greater than three solar masses collapses under its own gravity

Event horizon

Singularity (theoretical region of infinite density, pressure, and temperature)

SUPERNOVA

COLLAPSING STELLAR CORE

BLACK HOLE

25

The Solar System

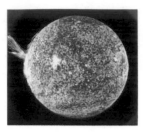

THE SUN

THE SOLAR SYSTEM consists of a central star (the Sun) and the bodies that orbit it. These bodies include nine planets and their 61 known moons, asteroids, comets, and meteoroids. The Solar System also contains interplanetary gas and dust. Most of the planets fall into two groups: four small rocky planets near the Sun (Mercury, Venus, Earth, and Mars), and four planets farther out, the gas giants (Jupiter, Saturn, Uranus, and Neptune). Pluto belongs to neither group—it is very small, solid, and icy. Pluto is the outermost planet, except when it passes briefly inside Neptune's orbit. Between the rocky planets and gas giants is the asteroid belt, which contains thousands of chunks of rock orbiting the Sun. Most of the bodies in the Solar System move around the Sun in elliptical orbits located in a thin disk around the Sun's equator. All the planets orbit the Sun in the same direction (counterclockwise when viewed from above) and all but Venus, Uranus, and Pluto also spin around their axes in this direction. Moons also spin as they, in turn, orbit their planets. The entire Solar System orbits the center of our galaxy, the Milky Way (see pp. 10-11).

(see pp. 10-11)

PLANETARY ORBIT

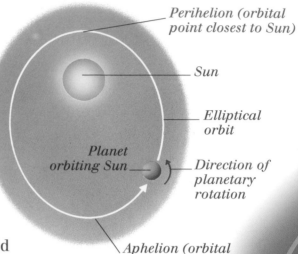

Perihelion (orbital point closest to Sun)

Sun

Elliptical orbit

Planet orbiting Sun

Direction of planetary rotation

Aphelion (orbital point farthest from Sun)

Aphelion of Neptune: 2,819 million miles

ORBITS OF INNER PLANETS

Average orbital speed of Venus: 21.8 miles/sec

Average orbital speed of Mercury: 29.8 miles/sec

Average orbital speed of Earth: 18.5 miles/sec

Average orbital speed of Mars: 15 miles/sec

Mercury

Perihelion of Mercury: 28.5 million miles

Perihelion of Venus: 66.7 million miles

Perihelion of Earth: 91.4 million miles

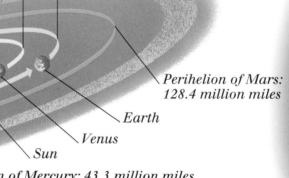

Mars

Perihelion of Mars: 128.4 million miles

Earth

Venus

Sun

Aphelion of Mercury: 43.3 million miles

Aphelion of Venus: 67.7 million miles

Asteroid belt

Aphelion of Earth: 94.5 million miles

Aphelion of Mars: 154.8 million miles

Aphelion of Pluto: 4,583 million miles

MERCURY
Year: 87.97 Earth days
Mass: 0.055 Earth masses
Diameter: 3,031 miles

VENUS
Year: 224.7 Earth days
Mass: 0.81 Earth masses
Diameter: 7,521 miles

EARTH
Year: 365.26 days
Mass: 1 Earth mass
Diameter: 7,926 miles

MARS
Year: 1.88 Earth years
Mass: 0.11 Earth masses
Diameter: 4,217 miles

JUPITER
Year: 11.86 Earth years
Mass: 318 Earth masses
Diameter: 88,850 miles

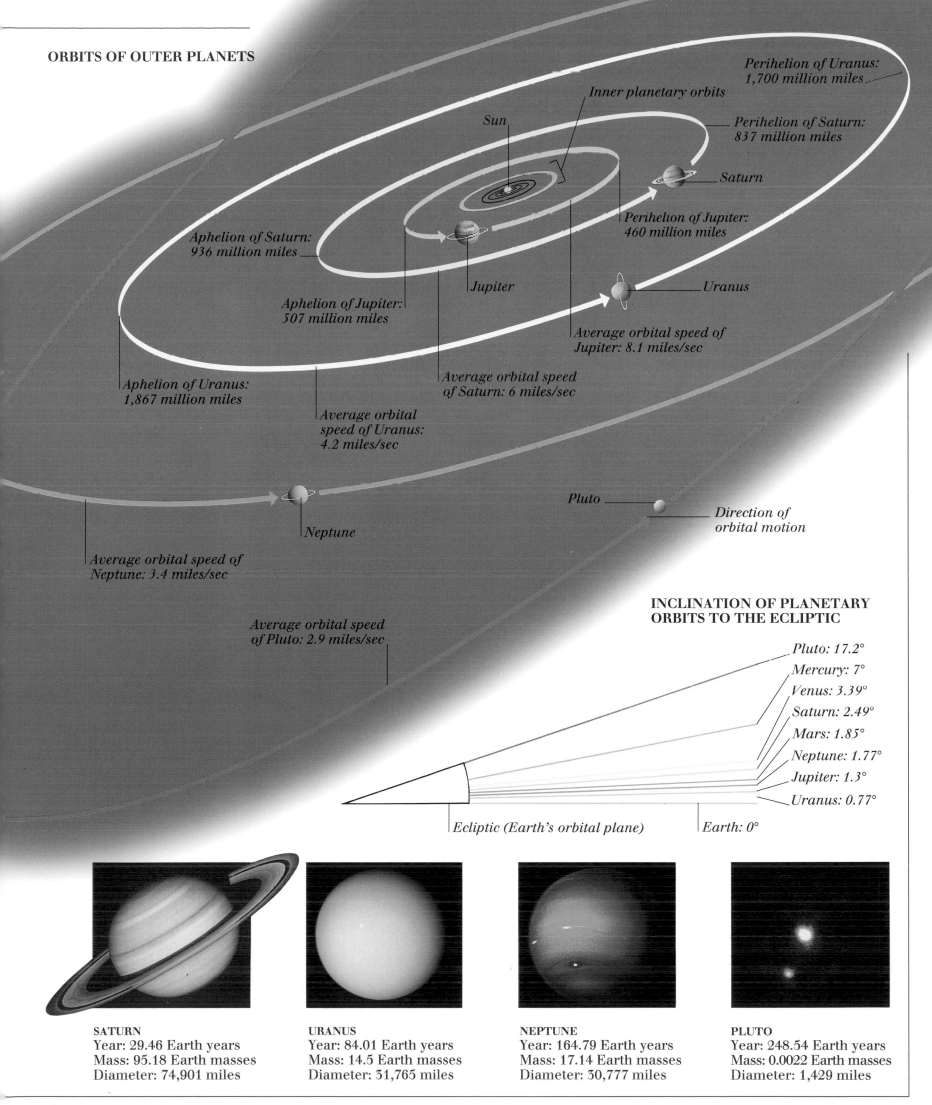

ORBITS OF OUTER PLANETS

Inner planetary orbits

Sun

Perihelion of Uranus:
1,700 million miles

Perihelion of Saturn:
837 million miles

Saturn

Perihelion of Jupiter:
460 million miles

Aphelion of Saturn:
936 million miles

Jupiter

Uranus

Aphelion of Jupiter:
507 million miles

Average orbital speed of
Jupiter: 8.1 miles/sec

Aphelion of Uranus:
1,867 million miles

Average orbital
speed of Uranus:
4.2 miles/sec

Average orbital speed
of Saturn: 6 miles/sec

Pluto

Direction of
orbital motion

Neptune

Average orbital speed of
Neptune: 3.4 miles/sec

INCLINATION OF PLANETARY
ORBITS TO THE ECLIPTIC

Average orbital speed
of Pluto: 2.9 miles/sec

Pluto: 17.2°
Mercury: 7°
Venus: 3.39°
Saturn: 2.49°
Mars: 1.85°
Neptune: 1.77°
Jupiter: 1.3°
Uranus: 0.77°

Ecliptic (Earth's orbital plane)   *Earth: 0°*

SATURN
Year: 29.46 Earth years
Mass: 95.18 Earth masses
Diameter: 74,901 miles

URANUS
Year: 84.01 Earth years
Mass: 14.5 Earth masses
Diameter: 31,765 miles

NEPTUNE
Year: 164.79 Earth years
Mass: 17.14 Earth masses
Diameter: 30,777 miles

PLUTO
Year: 248.54 Earth years
Mass: 0.0022 Earth masses
Diameter: 1,429 miles

The Sun

SOLAR PHOTOSPHERE

THE SUN IS THE STAR AT THE CENTER of our Solar System. It is about five billion years old and will probably continue to shine as it does now for about another five billion years. The Sun is a yellow main sequence star (see pp. 18-19) about 870,000 miles in diameter. It consists almost entirely of hydrogen and helium. In the Sun's core, hydrogen is converted to helium by nuclear fusion, releasing energy in the process. The energy travels from the core through the radiative and convective zones to the photosphere (visible surface), where it leaves the Sun in the form of heat and light. On the photosphere there are often dark, relatively cool areas called sunspots. These usually appear in pairs or groups and are thought to be caused by magnetic fields. Other types of solar activity are flares, which are usually associated with sunspots, and prominences. Flares are sudden discharges of high-energy radiation and atomic particles. Prominences are huge loops or filaments of gas extending into the solar atmosphere; some last for hours, others for months. Beyond the photosphere is the chromosphere (inner atmosphere) and the extremely rarified corona (outer atmosphere), which extends millions of miles into space. Tiny particles that escape from the corona give rise to the solar wind, which streams through space at hundreds of miles per second. The chromosphere and corona can be seen from Earth when the Sun is totally eclipsed by the Moon.

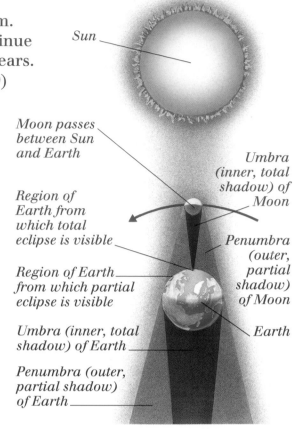

Sun

Moon passes between Sun and Earth

Umbra (inner, total shadow) of Moon

Region of Earth from which total eclipse is visible

Penumbra (outer, partial shadow) of Moon

Region of Earth from which partial eclipse is visible

Earth

Umbra (inner, total shadow) of Earth

Penumbra (outer, partial shadow) of Earth

SURFACE FEATURES

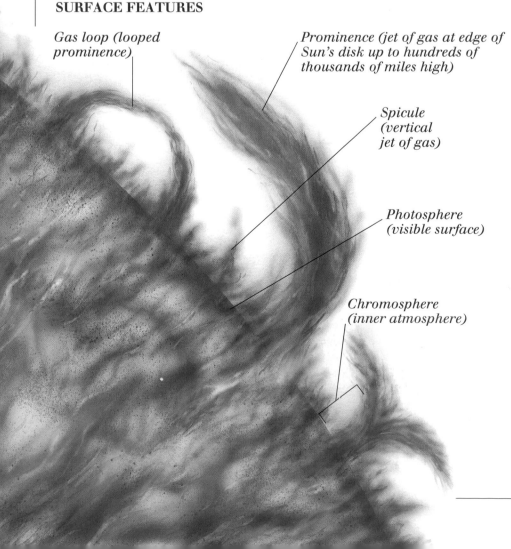

Gas loop (looped prominence)

Prominence (jet of gas at edge of Sun's disk up to hundreds of thousands of miles high)

Spicule (vertical jet of gas)

Photosphere (visible surface)

Chromosphere (inner atmosphere)

TOTAL SOLAR ECLIPSE

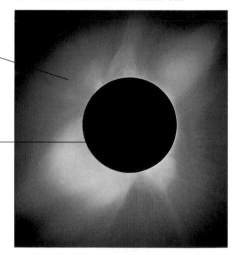

Corona (outer atmosphere of extremely hot diffuse gas)

Moon covers Sun's disk

SUNSPOTS

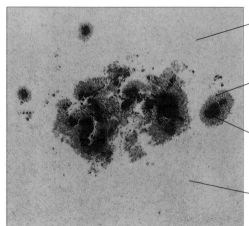

Granulated surface of Sun

Penumbra (lighter, outer region) containing radial fibrils

Umbra (darker, inner region) temperature about 7,200°F

Photosphere temperature about 9,900°F

EXTERNAL FEATURES AND INTERNAL STRUCTURE OF THE SUN

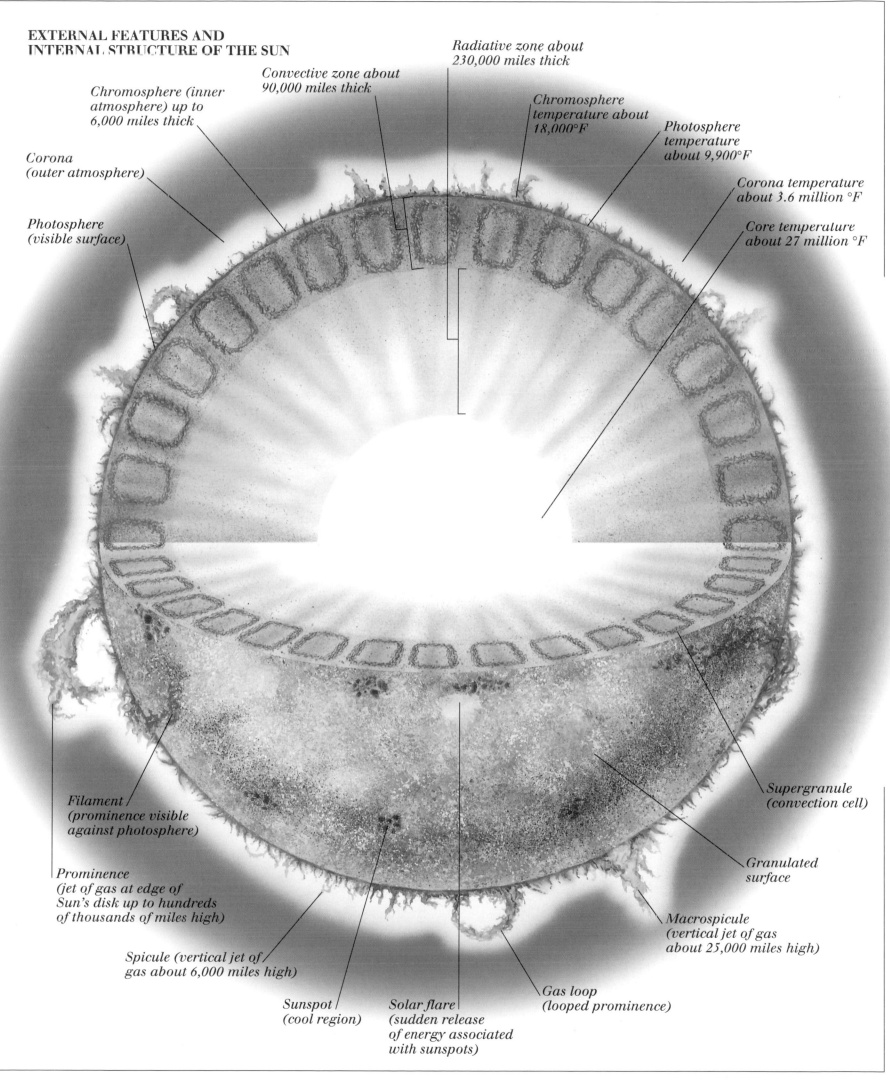

Chromosphere (inner atmosphere) up to 6,000 miles thick

Convective zone about 90,000 miles thick

Radiative zone about 230,000 miles thick

Chromosphere temperature about 18,000°F

Photosphere temperature about 9,900°F

Corona (outer atmosphere)

Corona temperature about 3.6 million °F

Core temperature about 27 million °F

Photosphere (visible surface)

Supergranule (convection cell)

Filament (prominence visible against photosphere)

Granulated surface

Prominence (jet of gas at edge of Sun's disk up to hundreds of thousands of miles high)

Macrospicule (vertical jet of gas about 25,000 miles high)

Spicule (vertical jet of gas about 6,000 miles high)

Sunspot (cool region)

Solar flare (sudden release of energy associated with sunspots)

Gas loop (looped prominence)

Mercury

MERCURY

MERCURY IS THE NEAREST PLANET to the Sun, orbiting at an average distance of about 36 million miles. Because Mercury is the closest planet to the Sun, it moves faster than any other planet, traveling at an average speed of nearly 30 miles per second and completing an orbit in just under 88 days. Mercury is very small (only Pluto is smaller) and rocky. Most of the surface has been heavily cratered by the impact of meteorites, although there are also smooth, sparsely cratered plains. The Caloris Basin is the largest crater, measuring about 800 miles across. It is thought to have been formed when a rock the size of an asteroid hit the planet and is surrounded by concentric rings of mountains thrown up by the impact. The surface also has many ridges, called rupes, that are thought to have been formed when the hot core of the young planet cooled and shrank about four billion years ago, buckling the planet's surface in the process. The planet rotates about its axis very slowly, taking nearly 59 Earth days to complete one rotation. As a result, a solar day (sunrise to sunrise) on Mercury is about 176 Earth days—twice as long as the 88-day Mercurian year. Mercury has extreme surface temperatures, ranging from a maximum of 800°F on the sunlit side to -270°F on the dark side. At nightfall, the temperature drops very quickly because the planet's atmosphere is almost nonexistent. It consists only of minute amounts of helium and hydrogen captured from the solar wind, plus traces of other gases.

TILT AND ROTATION OF MERCURY

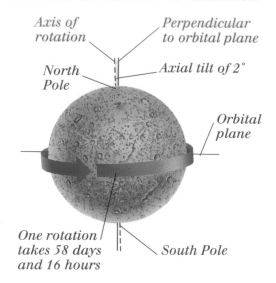

Axis of rotation

Perpendicular to orbital plane

North Pole

Axial tilt of 2°

Orbital plane

One rotation takes 58 days and 16 hours

South Pole

DEGAS AND BRONTË (RAY CRATERS)

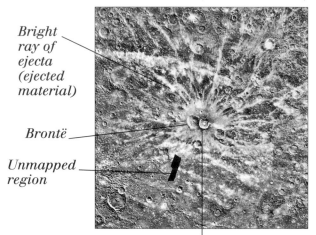

Bright ray of ejecta (ejected material)

Brontë

Unmapped region

Degas with central peak

FORMATION OF A RAY CRATER

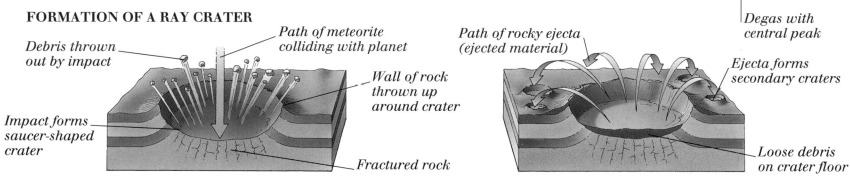

Debris thrown out by impact

Path of meteorite colliding with planet

Impact forms saucer-shaped crater

Wall of rock thrown up around crater

Fractured rock

METEORITE IMPACT

Path of rocky ejecta (ejected material)

Ejecta forms secondary craters

Loose debris on crater floor

SECONDARY CRATERING

Wall of rock forms ring of mountains

Ray of ejecta (ejected material)

Small secondary crater

Loose ejected rock

Central mountain rings form if floor of large crater recoils from meteorite impact

Falling debris forms ridges on side of wall

RAY CRATER

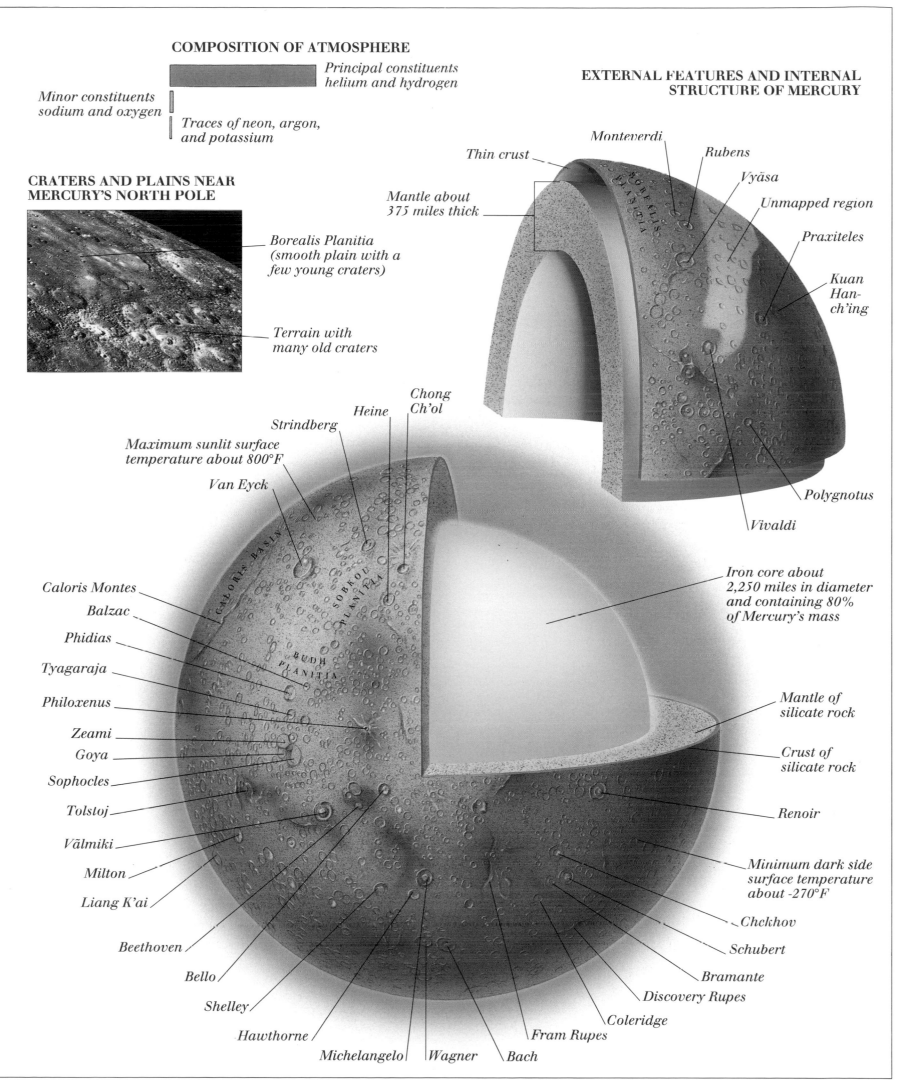

COMPOSITION OF ATMOSPHERE

Principal constituents helium and hydrogen

Minor constituents sodium and oxygen

Traces of neon, argon, and potassium

EXTERNAL FEATURES AND INTERNAL STRUCTURE OF MERCURY

CRATERS AND PLAINS NEAR MERCURY'S NORTH POLE

Borealis Planitia (smooth plain with a few young craters)

Terrain with many old craters

Thin crust

Mantle about 375 miles thick

Monteverdi

Rubens

Vyāsa

Unmapped region

Praxiteles

Kuan Han-ch'ing

Polygnotus

Vivaldi

Maximum sunlit surface temperature about 800°F

Van Eyck

Strindberg

Heine

Chong Ch'ol

Caloris Montes

Balzac

Phidias

Tyagaraja

Philoxenus

Zeami

Goya

Sophocles

Tolstoj

Vālmiki

Milton

Liang K'ai

Beethoven

Bello

Shelley

Hawthorne

Michelangelo

Wagner

Bach

Fram Rupes

Coleridge

Discovery Rupes

Bramante

Schubert

Chekhov

Minimum dark side surface temperature about -270°F

Renoir

Crust of silicate rock

Mantle of silicate rock

Iron core about 2,250 miles in diameter and containing 80% of Mercury's mass

31

Venus

RADAR IMAGE OF VENUS

VENUS IS A ROCKY PLANET and the second planet from the Sun. Venus spins slowly backward as it orbits the Sun, causing its rotational period to be the longest in the Solar System, at about 243 Earth days. It is slightly smaller than Earth and probably has a similar internal structure, consisting of a semisolid metal core surrounded by a rocky mantle and crust. Venus is the brightest object in the sky after the Sun and Moon because its atmosphere reflects sunlight strongly. The main component of the atmosphere is carbon dioxide, which traps heat in a greenhouse effect far stronger than that on Earth. As a result, Venus is the hottest planet, with a maximum surface temperature of about 900°F. The thick cloud layers contain droplets of sulfuric acid and are driven around the planet by winds at speeds of up to 220 miles per hour. Although the planet takes 243 Earth days to rotate once, the high-speed winds cause the clouds to circle the planet in only four Earth days. The high temperature, acidic clouds, and enormous atmospheric pressure (about 90 times greater at the surface than that on Earth) make the environment extremely hostile. However, orbiting satellites have managed to land on Venus and photograph its dry, dusty surface. The Venusian surface has also been mapped by probes with radar equipment that can "see" through the cloud layers. Such radar maps reveal a terrain with craters, mountains, volcanoes, and areas where craters have been covered by plains of solidified volcanic lava. There are two large highland regions called Aphrodite Terra and Ishtar Terra.

TILT AND ROTATION OF VENUS

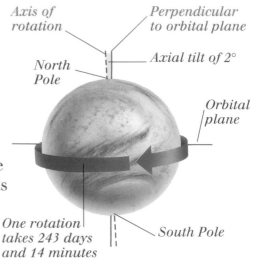

Axis of rotation

Perpendicular to orbital plane

Axial tilt of 2°

North Pole

Orbital plane

One rotation takes 243 days and 14 minutes

South Pole

CLOUD FEATURES

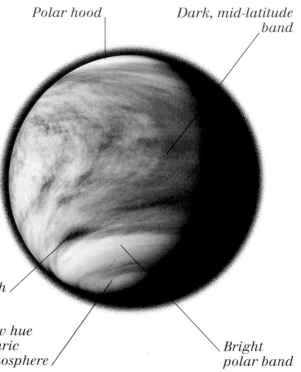

Polar hood

Dark, mid-latitude band

Cloud features swept around planet by winds of up to 220 mph

Dirty yellow hue due to sulfuric acid in atmosphere

Bright polar band

VENUSIAN CRATERS

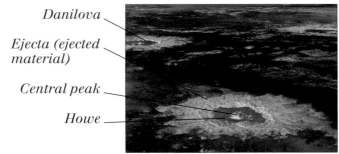

Danilova

Ejecta (ejected material)

Central peak

Howe

COMPUTER-ENHANCED RADAR MAP OF THE SURFACE OF VENUS

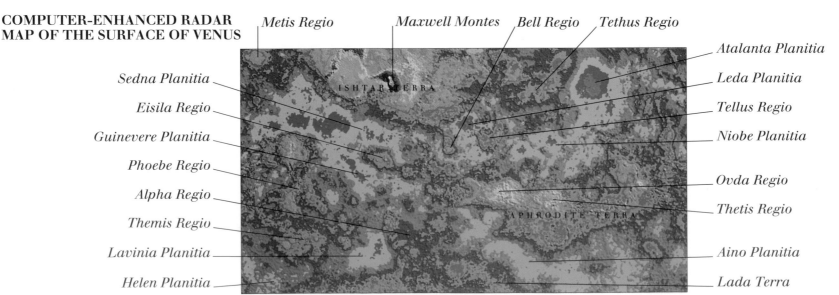

Metis Regio

Maxwell Montes

Bell Regio

Tethus Regio

Sedna Planitia

Eisila Regio

Guinevere Planitia

Phoebe Regio

Alpha Regio

Themis Regio

Lavinia Planitia

Helen Planitia

ISHTAR TERRA

APHRODITE TERRA

Atalanta Planitia

Leda Planitia

Tellus Regio

Niobe Planitia

Ovda Regio

Thetis Regio

Aino Planitia

Lada Terra

David A. Minich   May 26, 2000

Current Event Article

Venus

Venus is the second planet from the sun and is extremely rocky. Venus spins slowly backwards, 234 Earth days, as it orbits the sun. The main component of the atmosphere of Venus is carbon dioxide. This traps the heat in a greenhouse effect and as a result, we are able to see Venus from Earth with the naked eye. Venus is the hottest planet and often rains sulfuric acid. Orbiting satellites have managed to land on Venus and photograph its surface.

I picked this article because it had to do with space and what we have been talking about in class recently. I will read more articles just like this one because the book I got this article out of is my best science book. My goal is to have researched all the planets for my current even articles before the year is over, however I'm not sure if there will be enough time left.

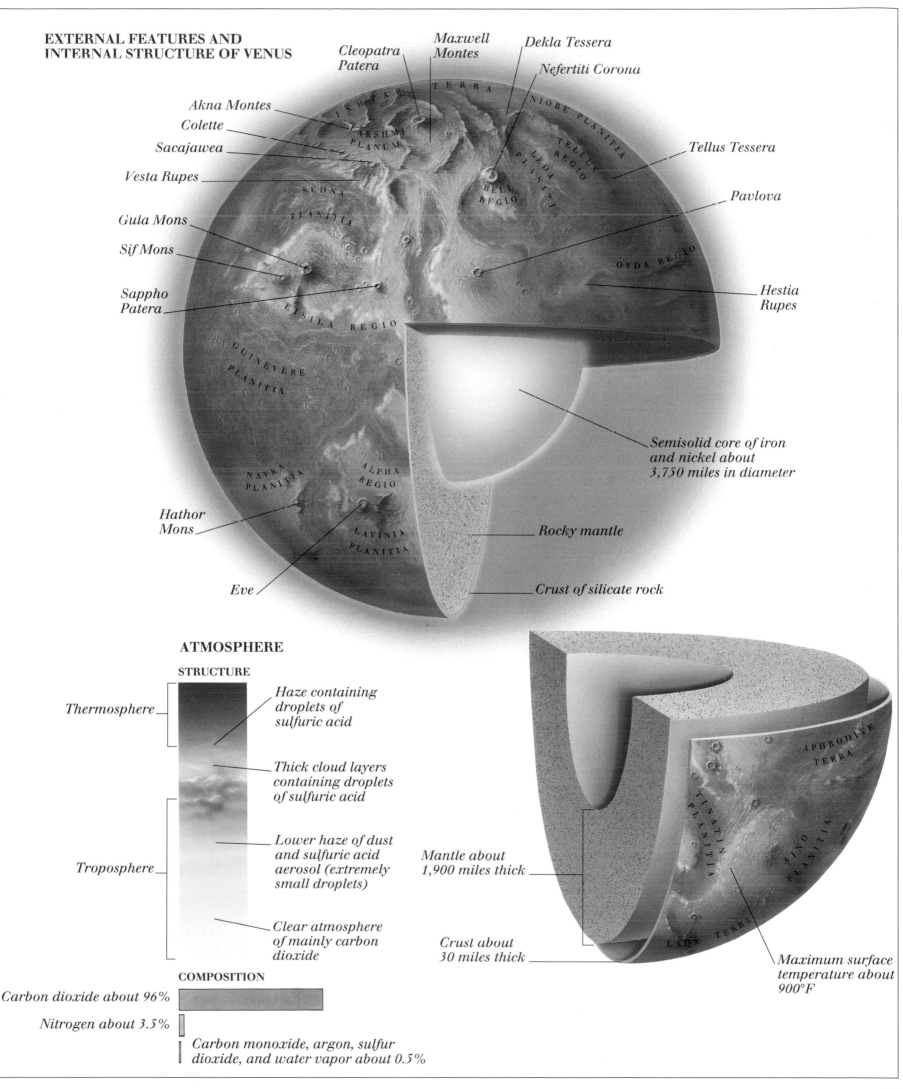

EXTERNAL FEATURES AND INTERNAL STRUCTURE OF VENUS

Cleopatra Patera

Maxwell Montes

Dekla Tessera

Nefertiti Corona

Akna Montes

Colette

Sacajawea

Vesta Rupes

Tellus Tessera

Gula Mons

Sif Mons

Pavlova

Sappho Patera

Hestia Rupes

Semisolid core of iron and nickel about 3,750 miles in diameter

Rocky mantle

Hathor Mons

Eve

Crust of silicate rock

ATMOSPHERE

STRUCTURE

Thermosphere

Haze containing droplets of sulfuric acid

Thick cloud layers containing droplets of sulfuric acid

Lower haze of dust and sulfuric acid aerosol (extremely small droplets)

Troposphere

Clear atmosphere of mainly carbon dioxide

Mantle about 1,900 miles thick

Crust about 30 miles thick

Maximum surface temperature about 900°F

COMPOSITION

Carbon dioxide about 96%

Nitrogen about 3.5%

Carbon monoxide, argon, sulfur dioxide, and water vapor about 0.5%

The Earth

EARTH

THE EARTH IS THE THIRD planet from the Sun, the largest and densest rocky planet, and the only planet known to support life. The Earth's interior of rock and metal is typical of a rocky planet, but its crust is unusual, consisting of separate plates that slowly move relative to each other. Earthquakes and volcanic activity occur along the boundaries where the plates collide. The Earth's atmosphere acts as a protective blanket by blocking out harmful radiation from the Sun and stopping meteorites from reaching the planet's surface, but trapping enough heat to prevent extremes of cold. About 70 percent of the Earth's surface is covered by water, which is not found in liquid form on the surface of any other planet. The Earth has one natural satellite, the Moon, which is large enough for both bodies to be considered a double-planet system.

TILT AND ROTATION OF THE EARTH

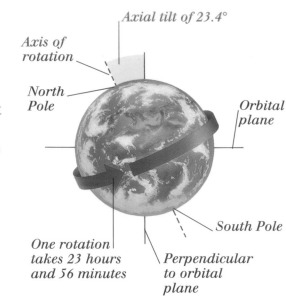

Axial tilt of 23.4°

Axis of rotation

North Pole

Orbital plane

One rotation takes 23 hours and 56 minutes

Perpendicular to orbital plane

South Pole

SATELLITE VIEWS OF THE EARTH (ATMOSPHERE NOT SHOWN)

North polar ice cap

Tundra

North America

Tropical rain forest

Amazon River

South America

Andes

Atlantic Ocean

Europe

Sahara

Tropical rain forest

Africa

Grassland and scrubland

Antarctica

Asia

Pacific Ocean

Himalayas

Tropical rain forest

Indian Ocean

Australia

Grassland and shrubland

Desert

Antarctica

TOPOGRAPHY OF THE EARTH'S CRUST

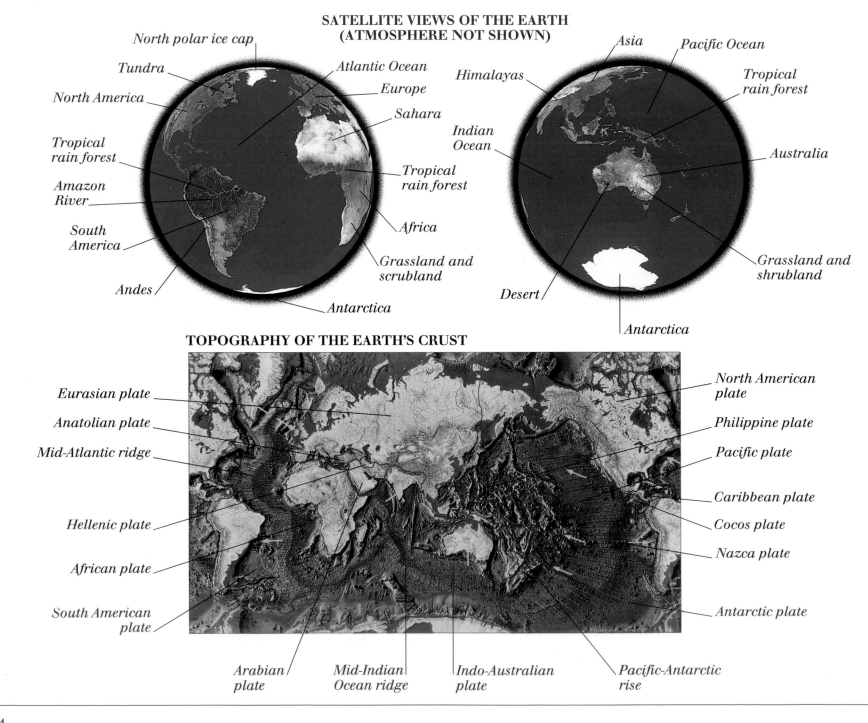

Eurasian plate

Anatolian plate

Mid-Atlantic ridge

Hellenic plate

African plate

South American plate

Arabian plate

Mid-Indian Ocean ridge

Indo-Australian plate

Pacific-Antarctic rise

North American plate

Philippine plate

Pacific plate

Caribbean plate

Cocos plate

Nazca plate

Antarctic plate

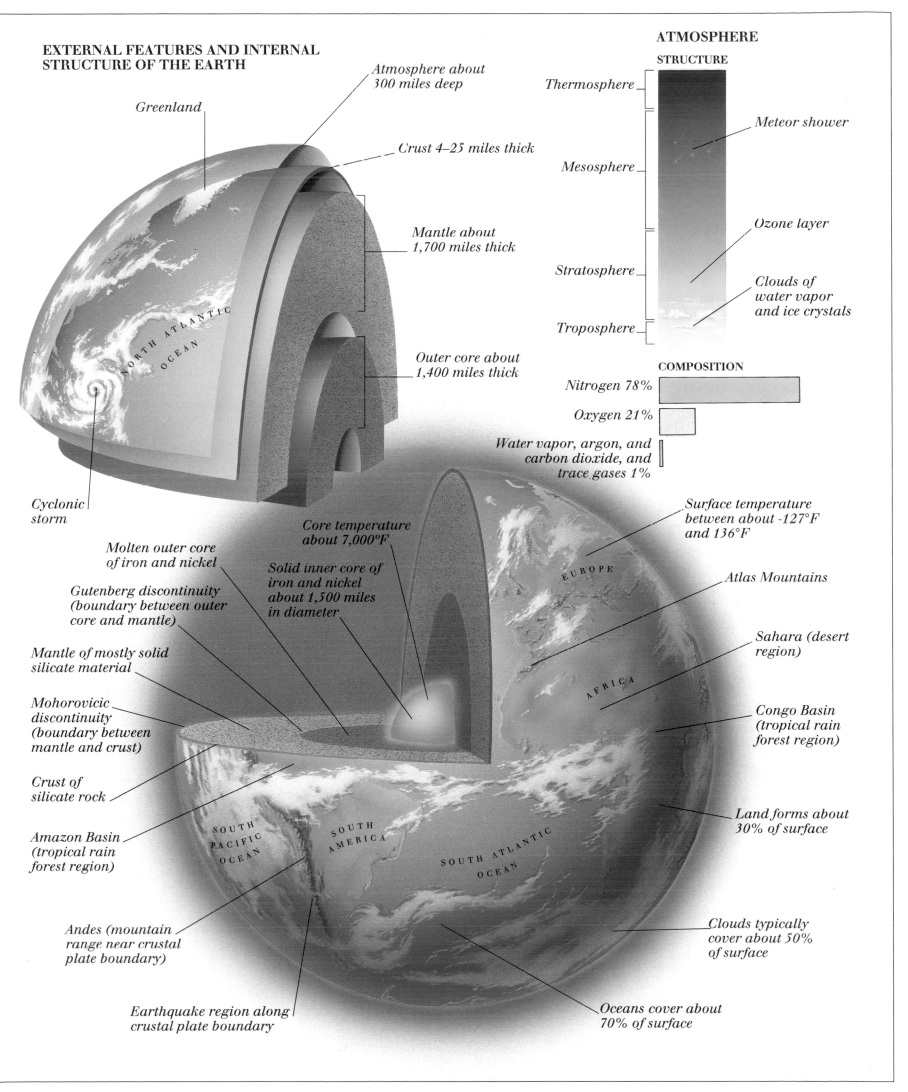

EXTERNAL FEATURES AND INTERNAL
STRUCTURE OF THE EARTH

Greenland

Atmosphere about
300 miles deep

Crust 4–25 miles thick

Mantle about
1,700 miles thick

NORTH ATLANTIC OCEAN

Outer core about
1,400 miles thick

Cyclonic
storm

ATMOSPHERE

STRUCTURE

Thermosphere

Mesosphere

Stratosphere

Troposphere

Meteor shower

Ozone layer

Clouds of
water vapor
and ice crystals

COMPOSITION

Nitrogen 78%

Oxygen 21%

Water vapor, argon, and
carbon dioxide, and
trace gases 1%

Core temperature
about 7,000°F

Molten outer core
of iron and nickel

Solid inner core of
iron and nickel
about 1,500 miles
in diameter

Gutenberg discontinuity
(boundary between outer
core and mantle)

Mantle of mostly solid
silicate material

Mohorovicic
discontinuity
(boundary between
mantle and crust)

Crust of
silicate rock

Amazon Basin
(tropical rain
forest region)

Andes (mountain
range near crustal
plate boundary)

Earthquake region along
crustal plate boundary

SOUTH
PACIFIC
OCEAN

SOUTH
AMERICA

SOUTH ATLANTIC
OCEAN

EUROPE

AFRICA

Surface temperature
between about -127°F
and 136°F

Atlas Mountains

Sahara (desert
region)

Congo Basin
(tropical rain
forest region)

Land forms about
30% of surface

Clouds typically
cover about 50%
of surface

Oceans cover about
70% of surface

The Moon

THE MOON FROM EARTH

THE MOON IS THE EARTH'S only natural satellite. It is relatively large for a moon, with a diameter of about 2,155 miles—just over a quarter that of the Earth. The Moon takes the same time to rotate on its axis as it takes to orbit the Earth (27.3 days), and so the same side (the near side) always faces us. However, the amount of the surface we can see—the phase of the Moon—depends on how much of the near side is in sunlight. The Moon is dry and barren, with no atmosphere or water. It consists mainly of solid rock, although its core may contain molten rock or iron. The surface is dusty, with highlands covered in craters caused by meteorite impacts, and lowlands in which large craters have been filled by solidified lava to form dark areas called maria or "seas." Maria occur mainly on the near side, which has a thinner crust than the far side. Many of the craters are rimmed by mountain ranges that form the crater walls and can be thousands of feet high.

TILT AND ROTATION OF THE MOON

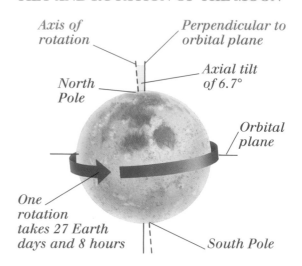

Axis of rotation

Perpendicular to orbital plane

Axial tilt of 6.7°

North Pole

Orbital plane

One rotation takes 27 Earth days and 8 hours

South Pole

CRATERS ON OCEANUS PROCELLARUM

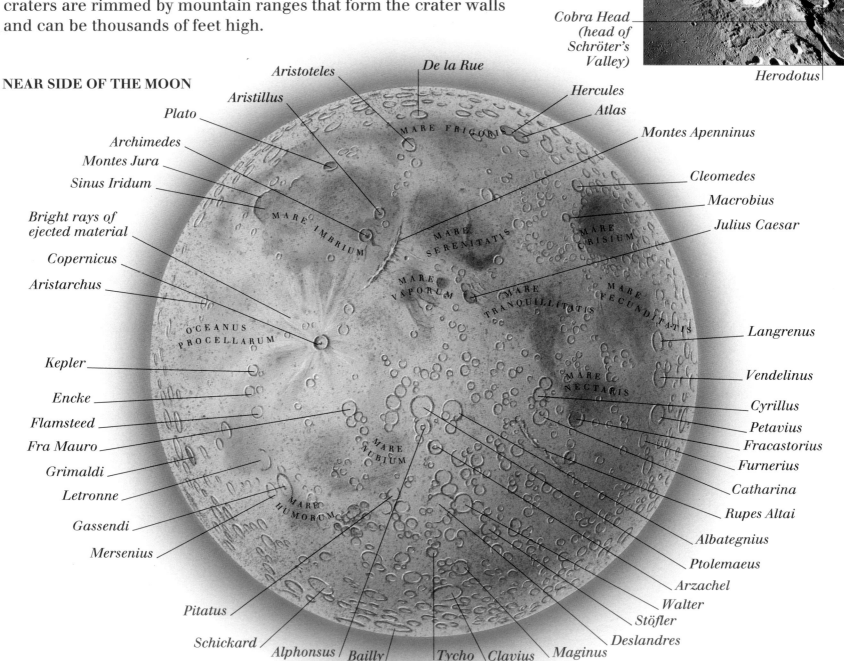

Aristarchus

Cobra Head (head of Schröter's Valley)

Herodotus

NEAR SIDE OF THE MOON

Aristoteles
De la Rue
Aristillus
Hercules
Plato
Atlas
Archimedes
Montes Apenninus
Montes Jura
Sinus Iridum
Cleomedes
Macrobius
Bright rays of ejected material
Julius Caesar
Copernicus
Aristarchus
Langrenus
Kepler
Vendelinus
Encke
Cyrillus
Flamsteed
Petavius
Fra Mauro
Fracastorius
Grimaldi
Furnerius
Letronne
Catharina
Gassendi
Rupes Altai
Mersenius
Albategnius
Ptolemaeus
Arzachel
Walter
Pitatus
Stöfler
Schickard
Deslandres
Alphonsus
Bailly
Tycho
Clavius
Maginus

MARE FRIGORIS
MARE IMBRIUM
MARE SERENITATIS
MARE CRISIUM
MARE VAPORUM
MARE TRANQUILLITATIS
MARE FECUNDITATIS
OCEANUS PROCELLARUM
MARE NECTARIS
MARE NUBIUM
MARE HUMORUM

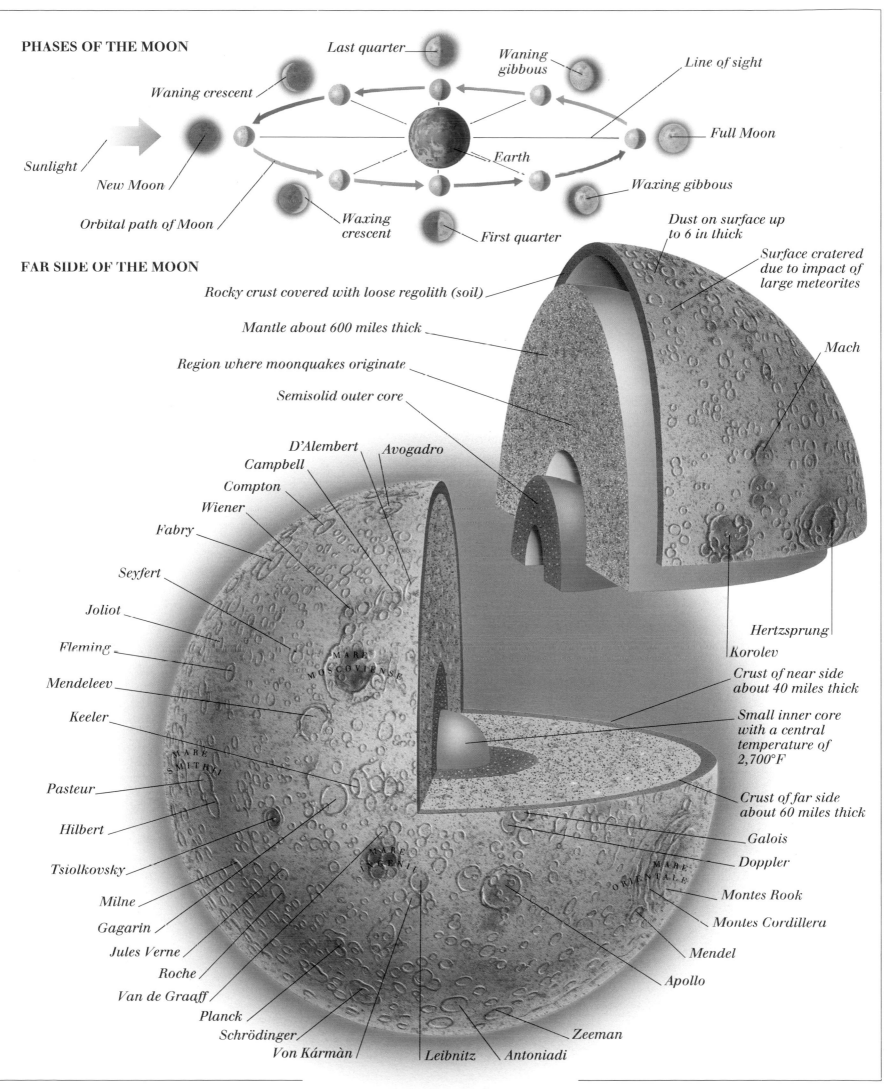

PHASES OF THE MOON

Last quarter

Waning crescent

Waning gibbous

Line of sight

Sunlight

Earth

Full Moon

New Moon

Orbital path of Moon

Waxing crescent

First quarter

Waxing gibbous

FAR SIDE OF THE MOON

Dust on surface up to 6 in thick

Surface cratered due to impact of large meteorites

Rocky crust covered with loose regolith (soil)

Mantle about 600 miles thick

Mach

Region where moonquakes originate

Semisolid outer core

D'Alembert

Avogadro

Campbell

Compton

Wiener

Fabry

Seyfert

Joliot

Fleming

Mendeleev

MARE MOSCOVIENSE

Keeler

Hertzsprung

Korolev

Crust of near side about 40 miles thick

Small inner core with a central temperature of 2,700°F

MARE SMITHII

Pasteur

Hilbert

Crust of far side about 60 miles thick

Galois

Doppler

Tsiolkovsky

MARE INGENII

MARE ORIENTALE

Montes Rook

Milne

Montes Cordillera

Gagarin

Jules Verne

Mendel

Roche

Van de Graaff

Apollo

Planck

Schrödinger

Von Kármàn

Leibnitz

Antoniadi

Zeeman

Mars

MARS

MARS, KNOWN AS THE RED PLANET, is the fourth planet from the Sun and the outermost rocky planet. In the 19th century, astronomers first observed what were thought to be signs of life on Mars. These signs included apparent canal-like markings on the surface, and dark patches that were thought to be vegetation. It is now known that the canals are an optical illusion and the dark patches are areas where the red dust that covers most of the planet has blown away. The fine dust particles are often whipped up by winds into dust storms that occasionally obscure almost all Mars's surface. Residual dust in the atmosphere gives the Martian sky a pinkish hue. The northern hemisphere of Mars has many large plains formed of solidified volcanic lava, while the southern hemisphere has many craters and large impact basins. There are also several huge, extinct volcanoes, including Olympus Mons, which at 370 miles wide and 15 miles high is the largest known volcano in the Solar System. The surface also has many canyons and branching channels. The canyons were formed by movements of the surface crust, but the channels are thought to have been formed by flowing water that has now vaporized almost completely and escaped from the atmosphere. The Martian atmosphere is much thinner than Earth's, with only a few clouds and morning mists. Mars has two tiny irregularly shaped moons, Phobos and Deimos. Their small size indicates that they may be asteroids that have been captured by the gravity of Mars.

TILT AND ROTATION OF MARS

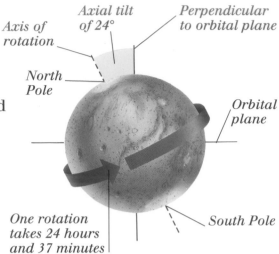

Axis of rotation

Axial tilt of 24°

Perpendicular to orbital plane

North Pole

Orbital plane

One rotation takes 24 hours and 37 minutes

South Pole

SURFACE FEATURES OF MARS

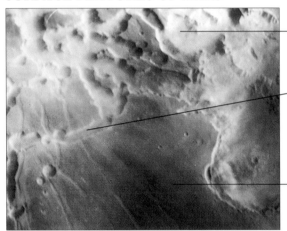

Bright water-ice fog

Fog in canyon about 12 miles wide at end of Valles Marineris

Syria Planum

NOCTIS LABYRINTHUS (CANYON SYSTEM)

Summit caldera consisting of overlapping collapsed volcanic craters

Crater

Gentle slope produced by lava flow

Cloud formation

OLYMPUS MONS (EXTINCT SHIELD VOLCANO)

THE SURFACE OF MARS

Dark area where dust has been blown away by wind

South polar ice cap

Surface covered with red-colored iron oxide dust

MOONS OF MARS

PHOBOS
Average diameter: 14 miles
Average distance from planet: 5,800 miles

DEIMOS
Average diameter: 8 miles
Average distance from planet: 14,600 miles

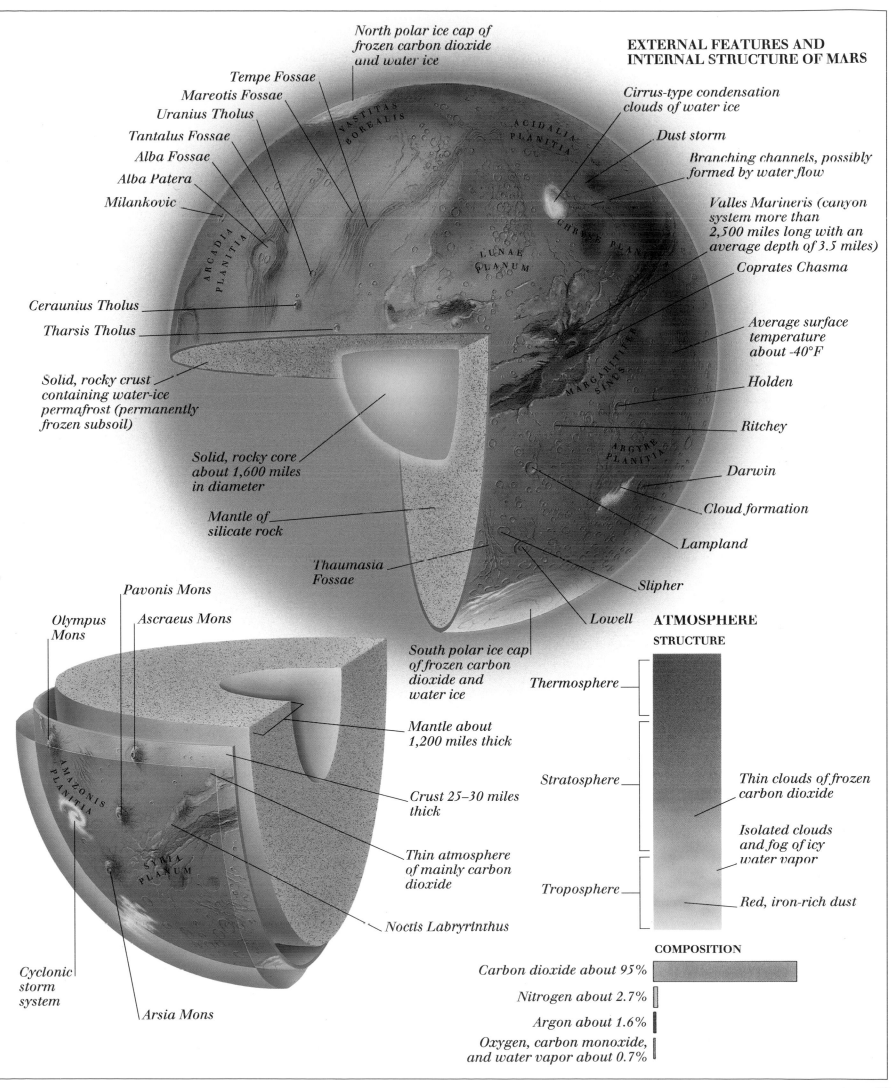

North polar ice cap of frozen carbon dioxide and water ice

Tempe Fossae

Mareotis Fossae

Uranius Tholus

Tantalus Fossae

Alba Fossae

Alba Patera

Milankovic

Ceraunius Tholus

Tharsis Tholus

Solid, rocky crust containing water-ice permafrost (permanently frozen subsoil)

Solid, rocky core about 1,600 miles in diameter

Mantle of silicate rock

Thaumasia Fossae

EXTERNAL FEATURES AND INTERNAL STRUCTURE OF MARS

Cirrus-type condensation clouds of water ice

Dust storm

Branching channels, possibly formed by water flow

Valles Marineris (canyon system more than 2,500 miles long with an average depth of 3.5 miles)

Coprates Chasma

Average surface temperature about -40°F

Holden

Ritchey

Darwin

Cloud formation

Lampland

Slipher

Lowell

South polar ice cap of frozen carbon dioxide and water ice

Olympus Mons

Pavonis Mons

Ascraeus Mons

Mantle about 1,200 miles thick

Crust 25–30 miles thick

Thin atmosphere of mainly carbon dioxide

Noctis Labryrinthus

Cyclonic storm system

Arsia Mons

ATMOSPHERE

STRUCTURE

Thermosphere

Stratosphere

Troposphere

Thin clouds of frozen carbon dioxide

Isolated clouds and fog of icy water vapor

Red, iron-rich dust

COMPOSITION

Carbon dioxide about 95%

Nitrogen about 2.7%

Argon about 1.6%

Oxygen, carbon monoxide, and water vapor about 0.7%

Jupiter

JUPITER

JUPITER IS THE FIFTH PLANET from the Sun and the first of the four gas giants. It is the largest and the most massive planet, with a diameter about 11 times that of the Earth and a mass about 2.5 times the combined mass of the eight other planets. Jupiter is thought to have a small rocky core surrounded by an inner mantle of metallic hydrogen (liquid hydrogen that acts like a metal). Outside the inner mantle is an outer mantle of liquid hydrogen and helium that merges into the gaseous atmosphere. Jupiter's rapid rate of rotation causes the clouds in its atmosphere to form belts and zones that encircle the planet parallel to the equator. Belts are dark, low-lying, relatively warm cloud layers. Zones are bright, high-altitude, cooler cloud layers. Within the belts and zones, turbulence causes the formation of cloud features such as white ovals and red spots, both of which are huge storm systems. The most prominent cloud feature is a storm called the Great Red Spot, which consists of a spiraling column of clouds three times wider than the Earth that rises about five miles above the upper cloud layer. Jupiter has one thin, faint, main ring, inside which is a halo ring of tiny particles extending toward the planet. There are 16 known Jovian moons. The four largest moons (called the Galileans) are Ganymede, Callisto, Io, and Europa. Ganymede and Callisto are cratered and probably icy. Europa is smooth and icy and may contain water. Io is covered in bright red, orange, and yellow splotches. This coloring is caused by sulfurous material from active volcanoes that shoot plumes of lava hundreds of miles above the surface.

TILT AND ROTATION OF JUPITER

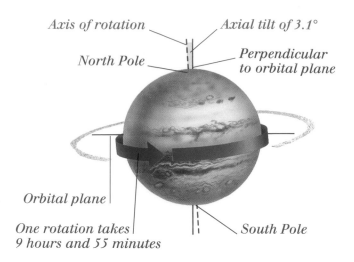

Axis of rotation

Axial tilt of 3.1°

North Pole

Perpendicular to orbital plane

Orbital plane

One rotation takes 9 hours and 55 minutes

South Pole

GREAT RED SPOT AND WHITE OVAL

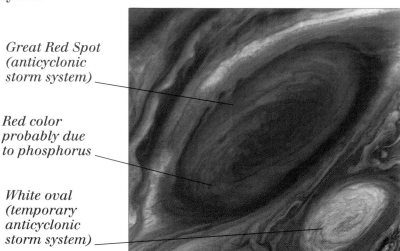

Great Red Spot (anticyclonic storm system)

Red color probably due to phosphorus

White oval (temporary anticyclonic storm system)

GALILEAN MOONS OF JUPITER

EUROPA
Diameter: 1,950 miles
Average distance from planet: 416,900 miles

CALLISTO
Diameter: 2,983 miles
Average distance from planet: 1,168,200 miles

GANYMEDE
Diameter: 3,270 miles
Average distance from planet: 664,900 miles

IO
Diameter: 2,263 miles
Average distance from planet: 262,100 miles

RINGS OF JUPITER

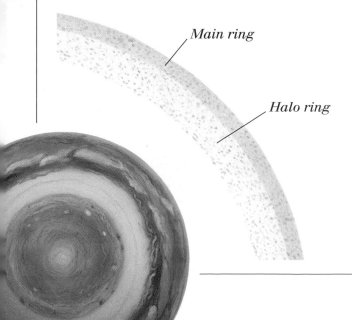

Main ring

Halo ring

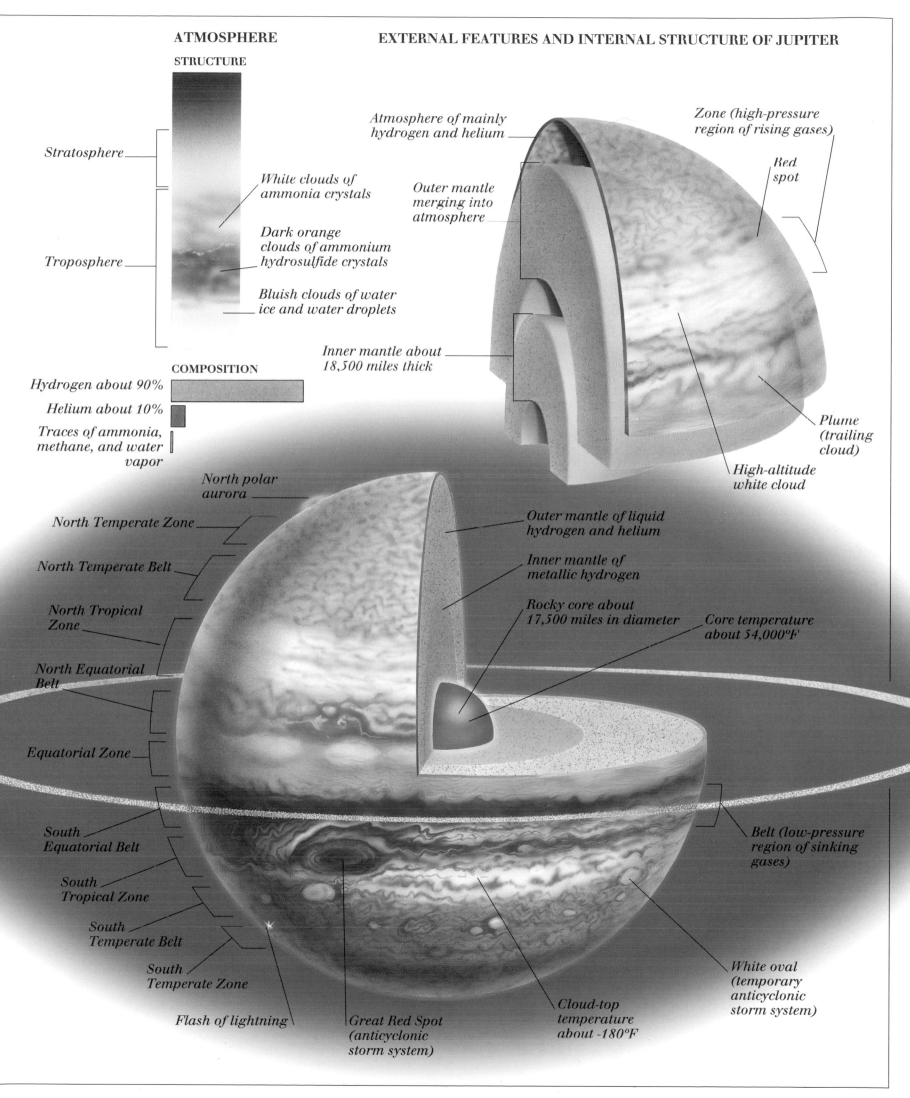

ATMOSPHERE

STRUCTURE

EXTERNAL FEATURES AND INTERNAL STRUCTURE OF JUPITER

Stratosphere

Troposphere

White clouds of ammonia crystals

Dark orange clouds of ammonium hydrosulfide crystals

Bluish clouds of water ice and water droplets

COMPOSITION

Hydrogen about 90%

Helium about 10%

Traces of ammonia, methane, and water vapor

Atmosphere of mainly hydrogen and helium

Outer mantle merging into atmosphere

Inner mantle about 18,500 miles thick

Zone (high-pressure region of rising gases)

Red spot

Plume (trailing cloud)

High-altitude white cloud

North polar aurora

North Temperate Zone

North Temperate Belt

North Tropical Zone

North Equatorial Belt

Equatorial Zone

South Equatorial Belt

South Tropical Zone

South Temperate Belt

South Temperate Zone

Flash of lightning

Great Red Spot (anticyclonic storm system)

Outer mantle of liquid hydrogen and helium

Inner mantle of metallic hydrogen

Rocky core about 17,500 miles in diameter

Core temperature about 54,000°F

Belt (low-pressure region of sinking gases)

White oval (temporary anticyclonic storm system)

Cloud-top temperature about -180°F

Saturn

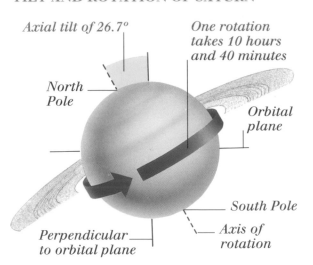

Axial tilt of 26.7°

One rotation takes 10 hours and 40 minutes

North Pole

Orbital plane

South Pole

Axis of rotation

Perpendicular to orbital plane

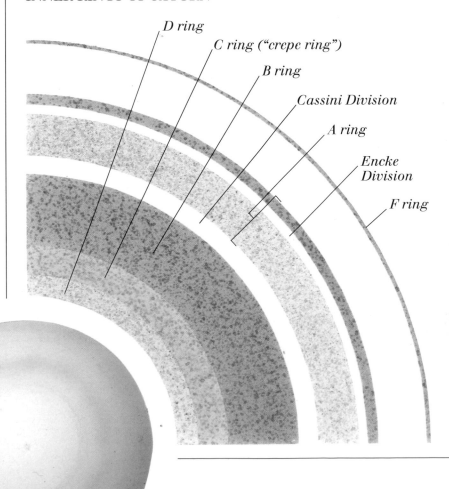

COLOR-ENHANCED IMAGE OF SATURN

SATURN IS THE SIXTH PLANET from the Sun. It is a gas giant almost as big as Jupiter, with an equatorial diameter of about 74,900 miles. Saturn is thought to consist of a small core of rock and ice surrounded by an inner mantle of metallic hydrogen (liquid hydrogen that acts like a metal). Outside the inner mantle is an outer mantle of liquid hydrogen that merges into a gaseous atmosphere. Saturn's clouds form belts and zones similar to those on Jupiter, but obscured by overlying haze. Storms and eddies, seen as red or white ovals, occur in the clouds. Saturn has an extremely thin but wide system of rings that is less than one mile thick but extends outward to about 260,000 miles from the planet's surface. The main rings comprise thousands of narrow ringlets, each made of icy lumps that range in size from tiny particles to chunks several yards across. The D, E, and G rings are very faint, the F ring is brighter, and the A, B, and C rings are bright enough to be seen from Earth with binoculars. Saturn has 18 known moons, some of which orbit inside the rings and are thought to exert a gravitational influence on the shapes of the rings. Unusually, seven of the moons are co-orbital—they share an orbit with another moon. Astronomers believe that such co-orbital moons may have originated from a single satellite that broke up.

COLOR-ENHANCED IMAGE OF SATURN'S CLOUD FEATURES

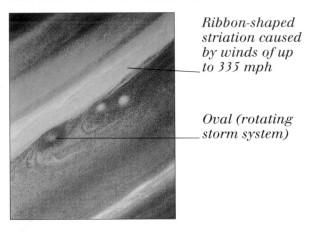

Ribbon-shaped striation caused by winds of up to 335 mph

Oval (rotating storm system)

INNER RINGS OF SATURN

D ring

C ring ("crepe ring")

B ring

Cassini Division

A ring

Encke Division

F ring

MOONS OF SATURN

ENCELADUS
Diameter: 309 miles
Average distance from planet: 148,000 miles

TETHYS
Diameter: 652 miles
Average distance from planet: 183,000 miles

DIONE
Diameter: 695 miles
Average distance from planet: 234,000 miles

MIMAS
Diameter: 247 miles
Average distance from planet: 115,600 miles

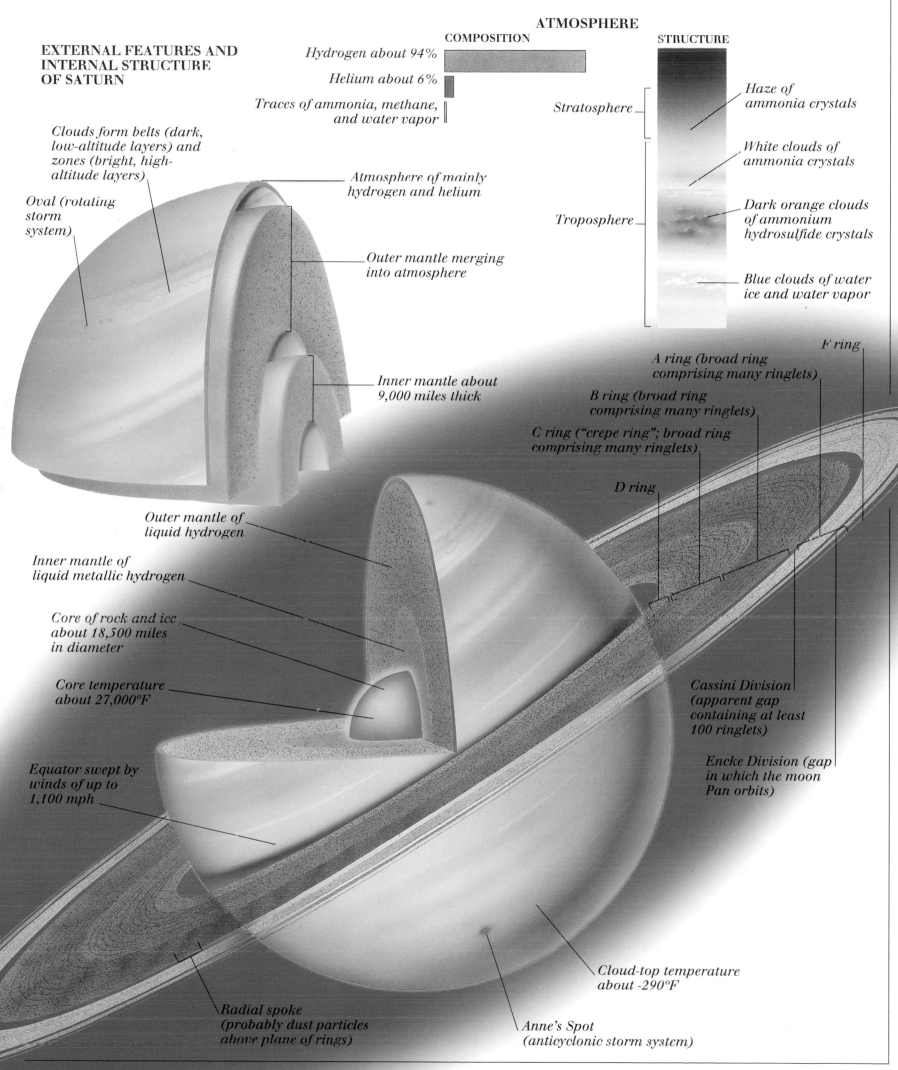

EXTERNAL FEATURES AND INTERNAL STRUCTURE OF SATURN

ATMOSPHERE

COMPOSITION

Hydrogen about 94%

Helium about 6%

Traces of ammonia, methane, and water vapor

STRUCTURE

Stratosphere

Troposphere

Haze of ammonia crystals

White clouds of ammonia crystals

Dark orange clouds of ammonium hydrosulfide crystals

Blue clouds of water ice and water vapor

Clouds form belts (dark, low-altitude layers) and zones (bright, high-altitude layers)

Oval (rotating storm system)

Atmosphere of mainly hydrogen and helium

Outer mantle merging into atmosphere

Inner mantle about 9,000 miles thick

Outer mantle of liquid hydrogen

Inner mantle of liquid metallic hydrogen

Core of rock and ice about 18,500 miles in diameter

Core temperature about 27,000°F

Equator swept by winds of up to 1,100 mph

A ring (broad ring comprising many ringlets)

B ring (broad ring comprising many ringlets)

C ring ("crepe ring"; broad ring comprising many ringlets)

D ring

F ring

Cassini Division (apparent gap containing at least 100 ringlets)

Encke Division (gap in which the moon Pan orbits)

Cloud-top temperature about -290°F

Radial spoke (probably dust particles above plane of rings)

Anne's Spot (anticyclonic storm system)

Uranus

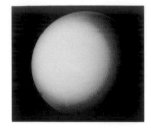

COLOR-ENHANCED IMAGE OF URANUS

URANUS IS THE SEVENTH PLANET from the Sun and the third largest, with a diameter of about 32,000 miles. It is thought to consist of a dense mixture of different types of ice and gas around a solid core. Its atmosphere contains traces of methane, giving the planet a blue-green hue, and the temperature at the cloud tops is about -350°F. Uranus is the most featureless planet to have been closely observed: only a few icy clouds of methane have been seen so far. Uranus is unique among the planets in that its axis of rotation lies close to its orbital plane. As a result of its strongly tilted rotational axis, Uranus rolls on its side along its orbital path around the Sun, while other planets spin more or less upright. Uranus is encircled by 11 rings that consist of rocks interspersed with dust lanes. The rings contain some of the darkest matter in the Solar System. They are extremely narrow, making them difficult to detect: nine of them are less than six miles wide, whereas most of Saturn's rings are thousands of miles in width. There are 15 known Uranian moons, all of which are icy and most of which are farther out than the rings. The 10 inner moons are small and dark, with diameters of less than 100 miles, and the five outer moons are between about 290 and 1,000 miles in diameter. The outer moons have a wide variety of surface features. Miranda has the most varied surface, with cratered areas broken up by huge ridges and cliffs 12 miles high.

TILT AND ROTATION OF URANUS

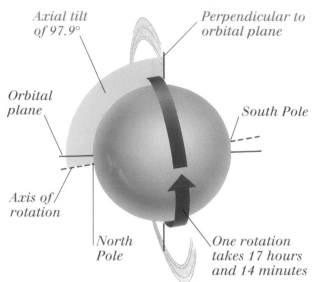

Axial tilt of 97.9°

Perpendicular to orbital plane

Orbital plane

South Pole

Axis of rotation

North Pole

One rotation takes 17 hours and 14 minutes

OUTER MOONS

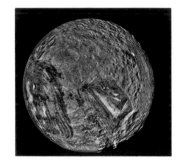

MIRANDA
Diameter: 293 miles
Average distance from planet: 80,700 miles

RINGS OF URANUS

Epsilon ring

Ring 1986 U1R

Delta ring

Gamma ring

Eta ring

Beta ring

Alpha ring

Rings 4 and 5

Ring 6

Ring 1986 U2R

RINGS AND DUST LANES

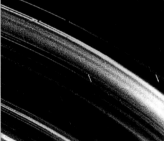

ARIEL
Diameter: 720 miles
Average distance from planet: 118,800 miles

TITANIA
Diameter: 981 miles
Average distance from planet: 270,900 miles

UMBRIEL
Diameter: 726 miles
Average distance from planet: 165,300 miles

OBERON
Diameter: 946 miles
Average distance from planet: 362,000 miles

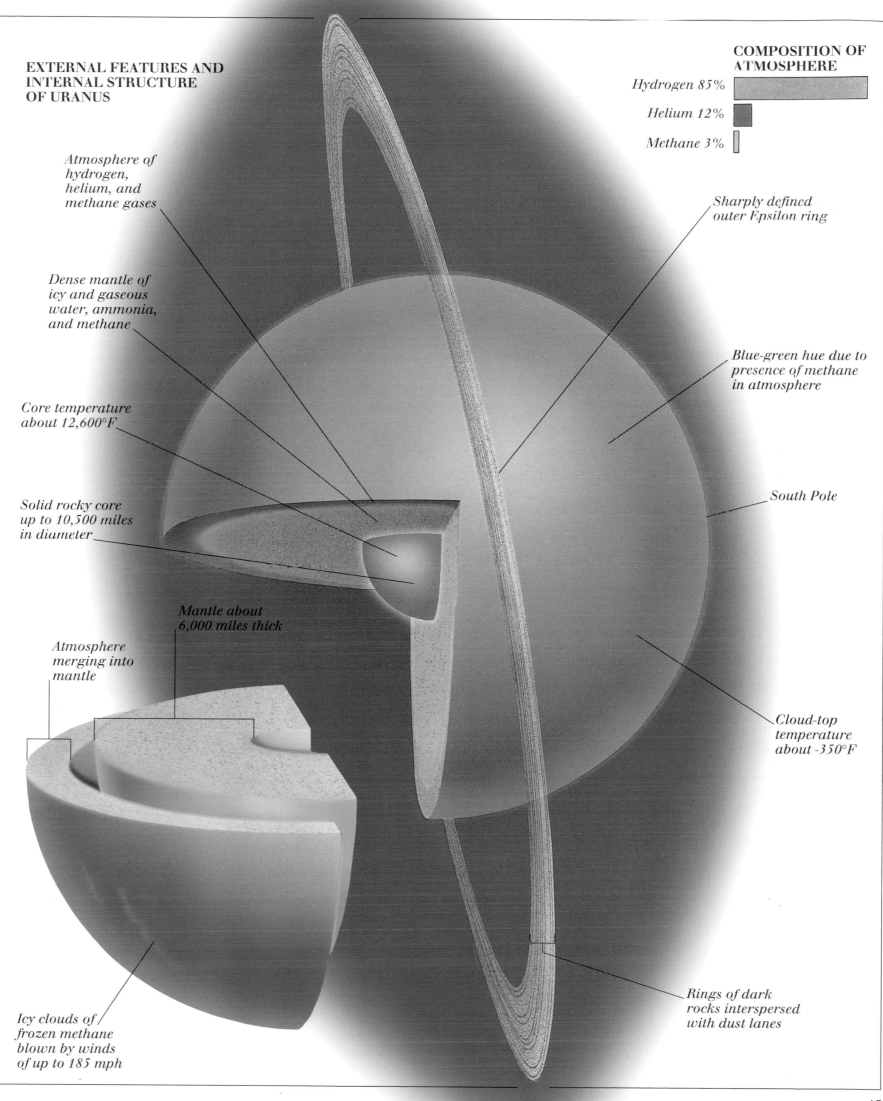

EXTERNAL FEATURES AND
INTERNAL STRUCTURE
OF URANUS

COMPOSITION OF
ATMOSPHERE

Hydrogen 85%

Helium 12%

Methane 3%

Atmosphere of
hydrogen,
helium, and
methane gases

Dense mantle of
icy and gaseous
water, ammonia,
and methane

Core temperature
about 12,600°F

Solid rocky core
up to 10,500 miles
in diameter

Mantle about
6,000 miles thick

Atmosphere
merging into
mantle

Icy clouds of
frozen methane
blown by winds
of up to 185 mph

Sharply defined
outer Epsilon ring

Blue-green hue due to
presence of methane
in atmosphere

South Pole

Cloud-top
temperature
about -350°F

Rings of dark
rocks interspersed
with dust lanes

45

Neptune and Pluto

COLOR-ENHANCED IMAGE OF NEPTUNE

NEPTUNE AND PLUTO are the two farthest planets from the Sun, at an average distance of about 2,800 million miles and 3,700 million miles, respectively. Neptune is a gas giant and is thought to consist of a small rocky core surrounded by a mixture of liquids and gases. The atmosphere contains several prominent cloud features. The largest of these are the Great Dark Spot, which is as wide as the Earth, the Small Dark Spot, and the Scooter. The Great and Small Dark Spots are huge storms that are swept around the planet by winds of about 1,200 miles per hour. The Scooter is a large area of cirrus cloud. Neptune has four tenuous rings and eight known moons. Triton is the largest Neptunian moon and the coldest object in the Solar System, with a temperature of -391°F. Unlike most moons in the Solar System, Triton orbits its mother planet in the opposite direction to the planet's rotation. Pluto is usually the outermost planet, but its elliptical orbit causes it to pass inside the orbit of Neptune for 20 years of its 248-year orbit. Pluto is so small and distant that little is known about it. It is a rocky planet, probably covered with ice and frozen methane. Pluto's only known moon, Charon, is large for a moon, at half the size of its parent planet. Because of the small difference in their sizes, Pluto and Charon are sometimes considered to be a double-planet system.

TILT AND ROTATION OF NEPTUNE

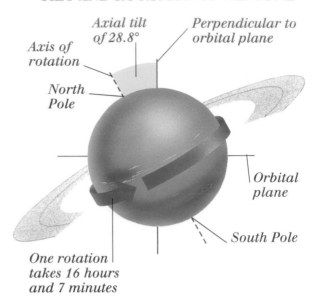

Axial tilt of 28.8°

Perpendicular to orbital plane

Axis of rotation

North Pole

Orbital plane

South Pole

One rotation takes 16 hours and 7 minutes

CLOUD FEATURES OF NEPTUNE

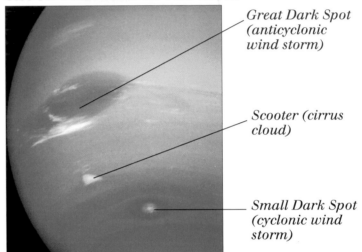

Great Dark Spot (anticyclonic wind storm)

Scooter (cirrus cloud)

Small Dark Spot (cyclonic wind storm)

HIGH-ALTITUDE CLOUDS

Methane cirrus clouds 25 miles above main cloud deck

Cloud shadow

Main cloud deck blown by winds at speeds of about 1,200 mph

RINGS OF NEPTUNE

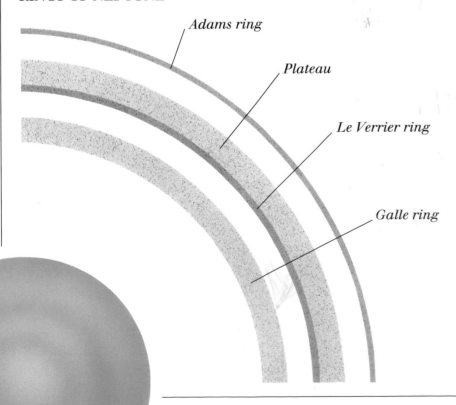

Adams ring

Plateau

Le Verrier ring

Galle ring

MOONS OF NEPTUNE

TRITON
Diameter: 1,681 miles
Average distance from planet: 220,500 miles

PROTEUS
Diameter: 259 miles
Average distance from planet: 73,100 miles

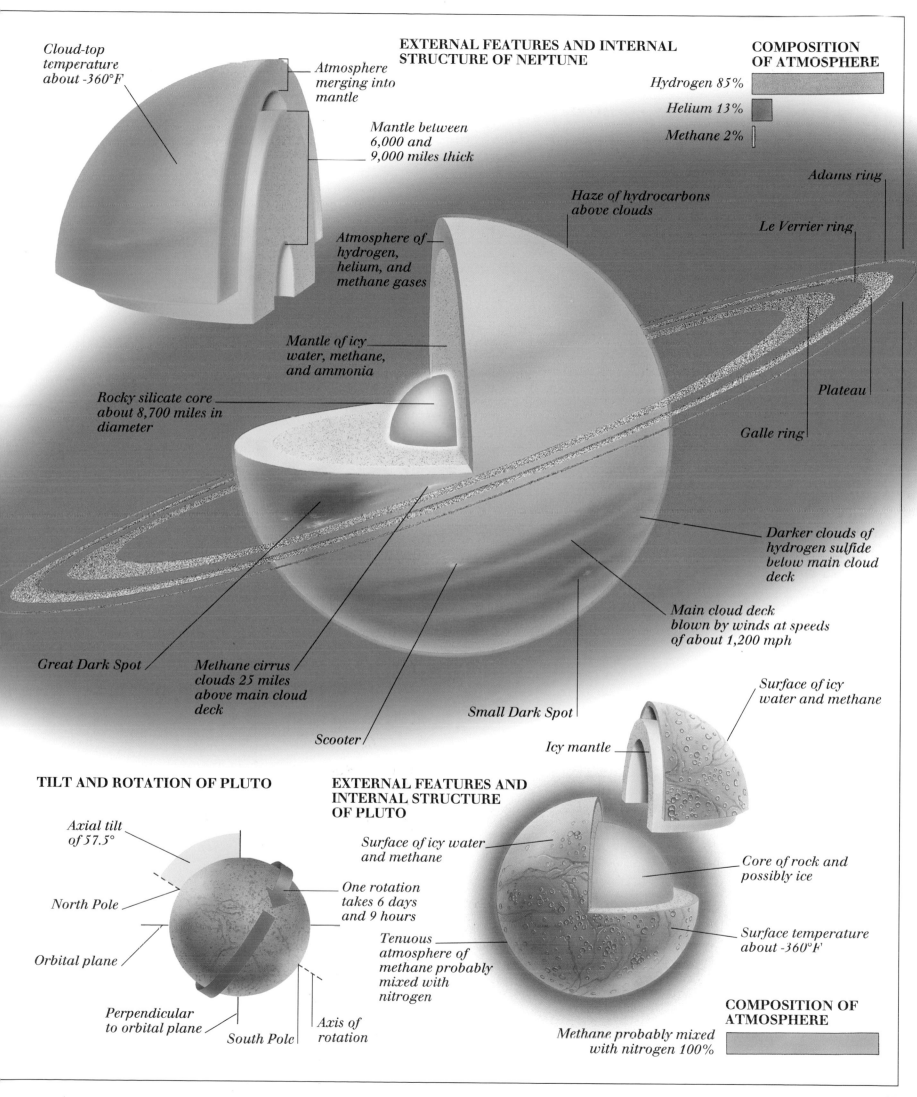

EXTERNAL FEATURES AND INTERNAL
STRUCTURE OF NEPTUNE

COMPOSITION
OF ATMOSPHERE

Hydrogen 85%

Helium 13%

Methane 2%

Cloud-top
temperature
about -360°F

Atmosphere
merging into
mantle

Mantle between
6,000 and
9,000 miles thick

Haze of hydrocarbons
above clouds

Adams ring

Le Verrier ring

Atmosphere of
hydrogen,
helium, and
methane gases

Mantle of icy
water, methane,
and ammonia

Rocky silicate core
about 8,700 miles in
diameter

Plateau

Galle ring

Darker clouds of
hydrogen sulfide
below main cloud
deck

Main cloud deck
blown by winds at speeds
of about 1,200 mph

Great Dark Spot

Methane cirrus
clouds 25 miles
above main cloud
deck

Scooter

Small Dark Spot

Surface of icy
water and methane

Icy mantle

TILT AND ROTATION OF PLUTO

EXTERNAL FEATURES AND
INTERNAL STRUCTURE
OF PLUTO

Axial tilt
of 57.5°

North Pole

Orbital plane

Perpendicular
to orbital plane

South Pole

Axis of
rotation

One rotation
takes 6 days
and 9 hours

Surface of icy water
and methane

Tenuous
atmosphere of
methane probably
mixed with
nitrogen

Core of rock and
possibly ice

Surface temperature
about -360°F

COMPOSITION OF
ATMOSPHERE

Methane probably mixed
with nitrogen 100%

Asteroids, comets, and meteoroids

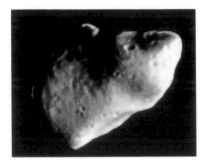

ASTEROID 951 GASPRA

ASTEROIDS, COMETS, AND METEOROIDS are all debris remaining from the nebula in which the Solar System formed 4.6 billion years ago. Asteroids are rocky bodies up to several hundred miles in diameter, although most are much smaller. Most of them orbit the Sun in the asteroid belt, which lies between the orbits of Mars and Jupiter. Comets may originate in a huge cloud, called the Oort Cloud, that is thought to surround the Solar System. They are made of frozen gases and dust, and are a few miles in diameter. Occasionally, a comet is deflected from the Oort Cloud to orbit the Sun in a long, elliptical path. As the comet approaches the Sun, the comet's surface starts to vaporize in the heat, producing a brightly shining coma (a huge sphere of gas and dust around the nucleus), a gas tail, and a dust tail. Meteoroids are small chunks of stone or stone and iron, some of which are fragments of asteroids or comets. Meteoroids range in size from tiny dust particles to objects tens of yards across. If a meteoroid enters the Earth's atmosphere, it is heated by friction and appears as a glowing streak of light called a meteor (also known as a shooting star). Meteor showers occur when the Earth passes through the trail of dust particles left by a comet. Most meteors burn up in the atmosphere. The few that are large enough to reach the Earth's surface are termed meteorites.

OPTICAL IMAGE OF HALLEY'S COMET

COLOR-ENHANCED IMAGE OF HALLEY'S COMET

High-intensity light emission

Nucleus

Medium-intensity light emission

Low-intensity light emission

COLOR-ENHANCED IMAGE OF A LEONID METEOR SHOWER

METEORITES

STONY METEORITE

Fusion crust formed when passing through atmosphere

Olivine and pyroxene mineral interior

STONY-IRON METEORITE

Iron

Stone (olivine)

DEVELOPMENT OF COMET TAILS

Dust tail deflected by photons in sunlight and curved due to comet's motion

Gas tail pushed away from Sun by charged particles in solar wind

Tails lengthen as comet nears Sun

Sun

Direction of comet's orbital motion

Coma surrounding nucleus

Tails behind nucleus

Tails in front of nucleus

Nucleus vaporized by Sun's heat, forming a coma with two tails

Gas tail

Dust tail

Coma and tails fade as comet moves away from Sun

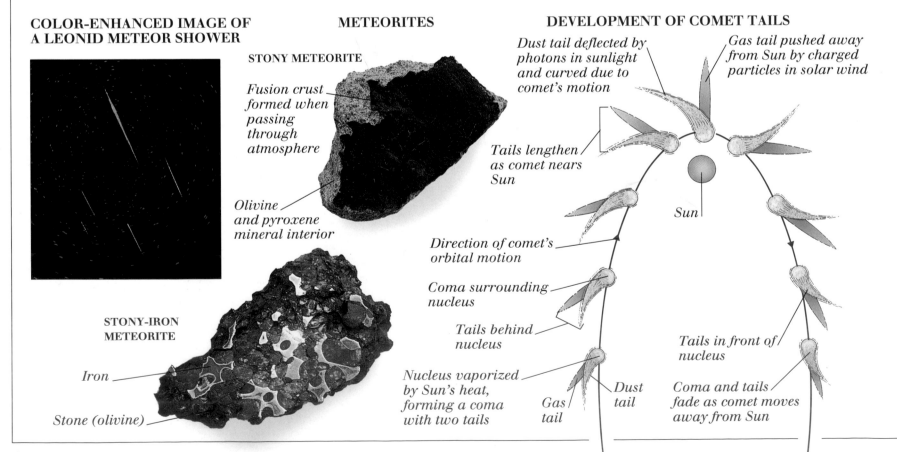

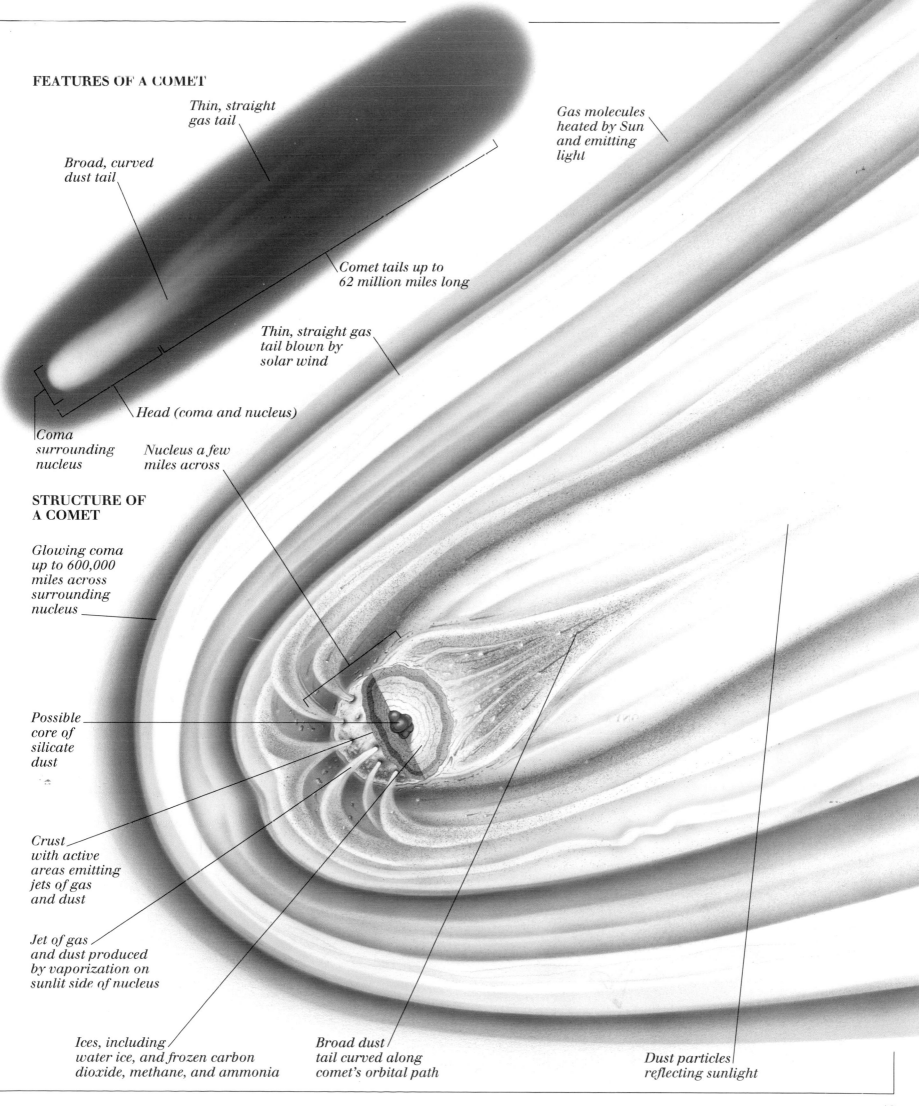

FEATURES OF A COMET

Thin, straight gas tail

Broad, curved dust tail

Gas molecules heated by Sun and emitting light

Comet tails up to 62 million miles long

Thin, straight gas tail blown by solar wind

Head (coma and nucleus)

Coma surrounding nucleus

Nucleus a few miles across

STRUCTURE OF A COMET

Glowing coma up to 600,000 miles across surrounding nucleus

Possible core of silicate dust

Crust with active areas emitting jets of gas and dust

Jet of gas and dust produced by vaporization on sunlit side of nucleus

Ices, including water ice, and frozen carbon dioxide, methane, and ammonia

Broad dust tail curved along comet's orbital path

Dust particles reflecting sunlight

Observing space

RADIO TELESCOPE

PEOPLE HAVE ALWAYS OBSERVED the stars, but it was not until the invention of the telescope in the 17th century that it was possible to see magnified images of celestial objects. There are three main types of telescope: reflectors, refractors, and radio telescopes. Reflectors and refractors are optical telescopes; they collect and magnify visible light. Reflectors use mirrors to collect the light, and refractors use lenses. The Hubble Space Telescope, which observes space from orbit, is a reflector. Space telescopes have the advantage of producing images that are undistorted by the Earth's atmosphere. Radiation from space that is absorbed by the Earth's atmosphere, such as some ultraviolet and infrared waves, can also be detected by some space telescopes. Radio telescopes collect radio waves emitted by celestial bodies and convert them into electrical signals, which are then used to produce images. Since the late 1950s, space probes have explored the Solar System. In 1971, the Soviet probe Mars 3 orbited Mars, transmitted pictures, and landed a capsule on the surface (although a dust storm rendered the capsule's instruments inactive). The U.S. Viking probes to Mars were more sophisticated: they obtained weather data, photographed the terrain, and tested the soil. The U.S. probe Voyager 2 has observed Jupiter, Saturn, Uranus, and Neptune and will continue to transmit data as it travels out of the Solar System.

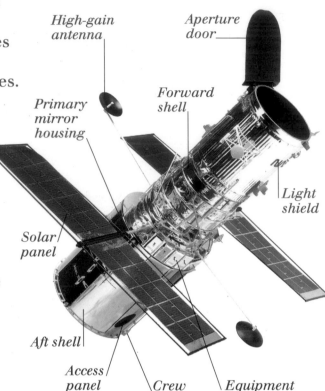

High-gain antenna

Aperture door

Primary mirror housing

Forward shell

Solar panel

Light shield

Aft shell

Access panel

Crew handrail

Equipment box

HOW TELESCOPES WORK

REFRACTOR

Objective lens

Incident light ray

Telescope tube

Refracted light ray

Eyepiece lens

REFLECTOR

Incident light ray

Eyepiece lens

Telescope tube

Primary mirror

Secondary mirror

Reflected light ray

SMALL REFRACTOR TELESCOPE

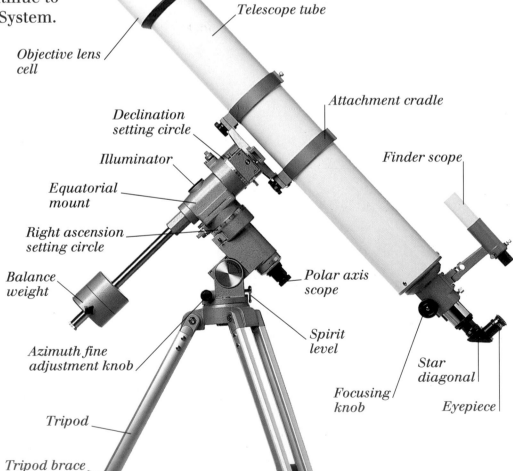

Telescope tube

Objective lens cell

Attachment cradle

Declination setting circle

Finder scope

Illuminator

Equatorial mount

Right ascension setting circle

Balance weight

Polar axis scope

Azimuth fine adjustment knob

Spirit level

Star diagonal

Tripod

Focusing knob

Eyepiece

Tripod brace

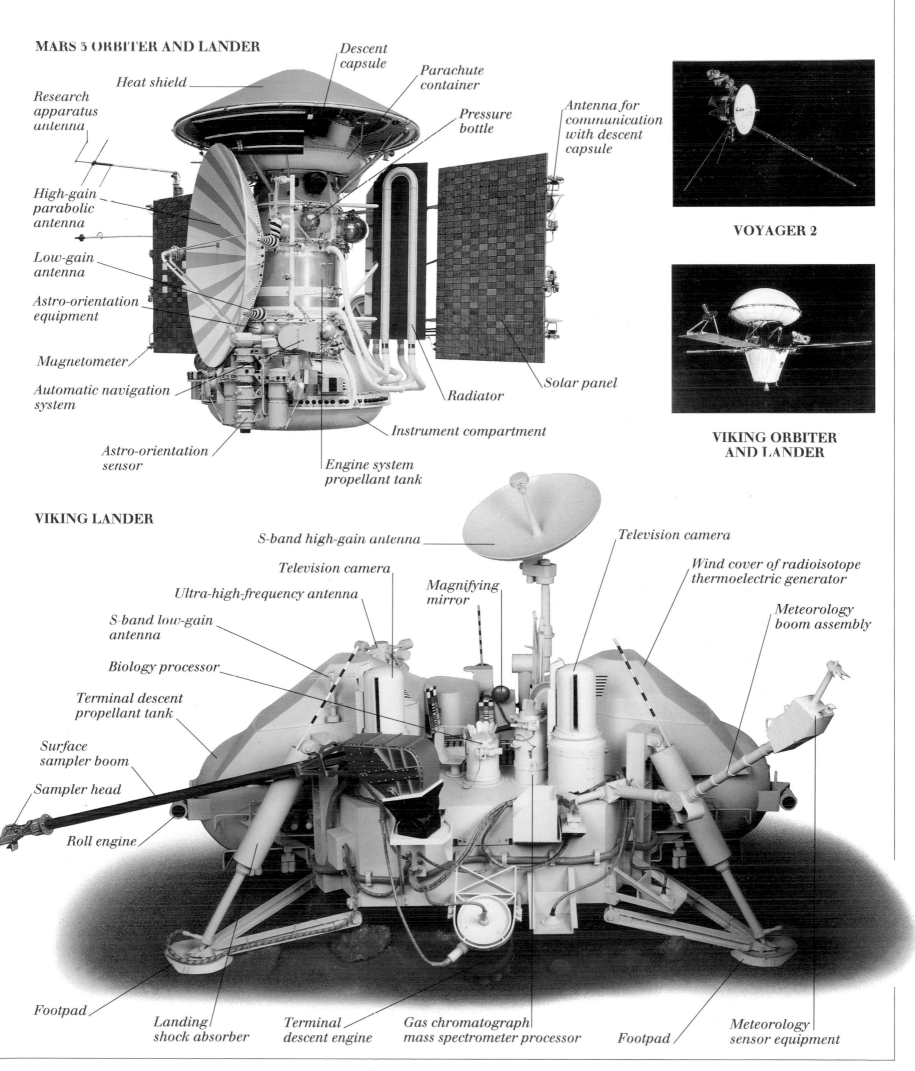

MARS 3 ORBITER AND LANDER

Research apparatus antenna

Heat shield

Descent capsule

Parachute container

Pressure bottle

Antenna for communication with descent capsule

High-gain parabolic antenna

Low-gain antenna

Astro-orientation equipment

Magnetometer

Automatic navigation system

Astro-orientation sensor

Engine system propellant tank

Instrument compartment

Radiator

Solar panel

VOYAGER 2

VIKING ORBITER AND LANDER

VIKING LANDER

S-band high-gain antenna

Television camera

Ultra-high-frequency antenna

Magnifying mirror

Television camera

Wind cover of radioisotope thermoelectric generator

S-band low-gain antenna

Biology processor

Meteorology boom assembly

Terminal descent propellant tank

Surface sampler boom

Sampler head

Roll engine

Footpad

Landing shock absorber

Terminal descent engine

Gas chromatograph mass spectrometer processor

Footpad

Meteorology sensor equipment

51

Manned space exploration

THE FIRST PERSON IN SPACE was the Soviet cosmonaut Yuri Gagarin, who completed one orbit of the Earth in his capsule Vostok 1 on April 12, 1961. For astronauts to survive in the hostile conditions of space, they must be provided with an artificial environment inside a spacesuit or spacecraft. Artificial environments provide astronauts with pressure and a breathable atmosphere, protect them from radiation and micrometeoroids, and regulate their body temperature. When exploring open space or the lunar surface, astronauts connect a portable life-support system (PLSS) to their spacesuit. The U.S. Space Shuttle is probably the most significant recent development in manned space exploration because it is reusable. Only the external fuel tank is lost on each mission; the solid rocket boosters are retrieved, and the orbiter glides back to Earth. The Shuttle has a large cargo bay, and a remote-controlled robotic arm that is used to launch, retrieve, and repair satellites in space. The cargo bay can carry a spacelab or components for a space station. Space stations have also played an important role in the recent manned exploration of space, and the development of space stations such as Skylab (U.S.) and Mir (U.S.S.R.) has shown that astronauts can live and work in space for months or even years. The U.S. Apollo lunar missions demonstrated that it is feasible to send humans to the Moon (see pp. 54-55). The next step is to send manned spacecraft to explore the planets, although it may take decades for this to be achieved.

SPACE SHUTTLE LIFTOFF

VOSTOK 1

- Gas pressure bottle for life-support system
- Securing band
- Communications antenna
- Radio command link antenna
- Reentry module containing ejection seat
- Equipment module
- Final stage of launch vehicle
- VHF antenna
- Final-stage engine
- Radio whip antenna
- Telemetry antenna
- Pitch and yaw control engine
- Radiator

SPACE SHUTTLE IN FLIGHT

SPACE SHUTTLE

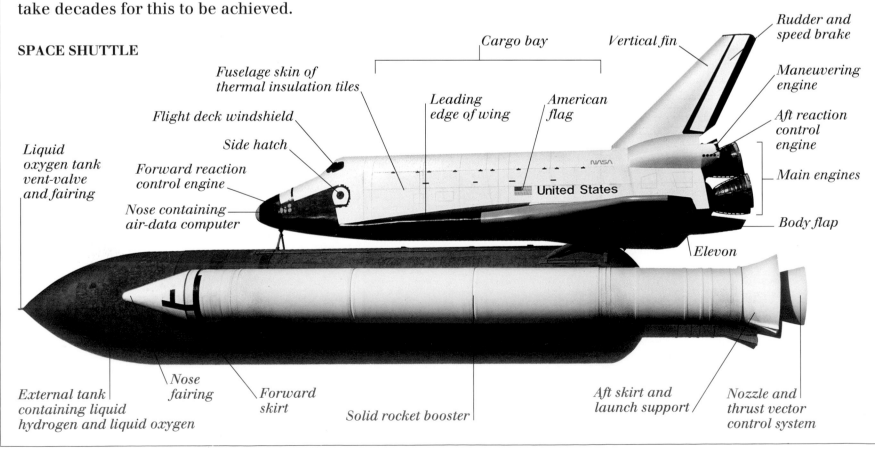

- Cargo bay
- Fuselage skin of thermal insulation tiles
- Flight deck windshield
- Side hatch
- Forward reaction control engine
- Nose containing air-data computer
- Liquid oxygen tank vent-valve and fairing
- Leading edge of wing
- American flag
- United States
- Vertical fin
- Rudder and speed brake
- Maneuvering engine
- Aft reaction control engine
- Main engines
- Body flap
- Elevon
- External tank containing liquid hydrogen and liquid oxygen
- Nose fairing
- Forward skirt
- Solid rocket booster
- Aft skirt and launch support
- Nozzle and thrust vector control system

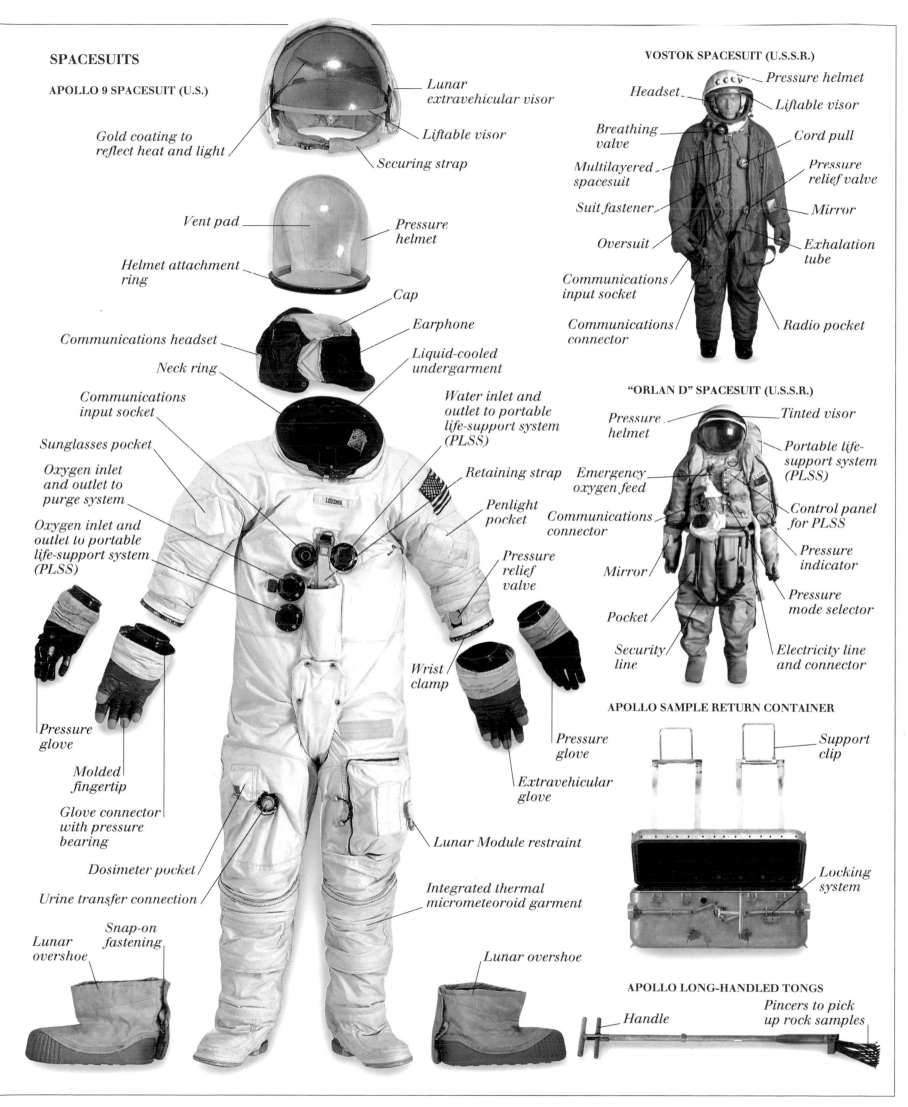

SPACESUITS

APOLLO 9 SPACESUIT (U.S.)

Lunar extravehicular visor

Gold coating to reflect heat and light

Liftable visor

Securing strap

Vent pad

Pressure helmet

Helmet attachment ring

Cap

Communications headset

Earphone

Neck ring

Liquid-cooled undergarment

Communications input socket

Water inlet and outlet to portable life-support system (PLSS)

Sunglasses pocket

Retaining strap

Oxygen inlet and outlet to purge system

Penlight pocket

Oxygen inlet and outlet to portable life-support system (PLSS)

Pressure relief valve

Pressure glove

Molded fingertip

Glove connector with pressure bearing

Dosimeter pocket

Urine transfer connection

Wrist clamp

Pressure glove

Extravehicular glove

Lunar Module restraint

Integrated thermal micrometeoroid garment

Snap-on fastening

Lunar overshoe

Lunar overshoe

VOSTOK SPACESUIT (U.S.S.R.)

Pressure helmet

Headset

Liftable visor

Breathing valve

Cord pull

Multilayered spacesuit

Pressure relief valve

Suit fastener

Mirror

Oversuit

Exhalation tube

Communications input socket

Communications connector

Radio pocket

"ORLAN D" SPACESUIT (U.S.S.R.)

Pressure helmet

Tinted visor

Portable life-support system (PLSS)

Emergency oxygen feed

Communications connector

Control panel for PLSS

Pressure indicator

Mirror

Pressure mode selector

Pocket

Security line

Electricity line and connector

APOLLO SAMPLE RETURN CONTAINER

Support clip

Locking system

APOLLO LONG-HANDLED TONGS

Handle

Pincers to pick up rock samples

53

Lunar exploration

APOLLO 11 LIFTOFF

THE MOON IS THE NEAREST celestial body to Earth, but until relatively recently little was known about it. Extensive exploration was first undertaken by unmanned probes. The Soviet Luna 2 was the first probe to reach the Moon, in 1959, and in 1966 Luna 9 transmitted the first pictures from the Moon's surface. One of the most sophisticated unmanned lunar probes was the remote-controlled Soviet vehicle Lunokhod 1, which traveled over the lunar surface taking television pictures and testing the soil. The first men landed on the Moon as part of the U.S. Apollo 11 mission on July 20, 1969. Apollo 11 had three components: a command module, a service module, and a lunar module. After going into orbit round the Moon, the lunar module descended to the Moon's surface with two astronauts (Neil Armstrong and Edwin "Buzz" Aldrin) on board. The astronauts took photographs, collected rock samples, and set up research equipment. They took off from the Moon in the module's ascent stage and docked with the command module before traveling the 238,855 miles back to Earth. Ten more American astronauts explored the Moon before the Apollo program ended in 1972. Since then, only a small number of unmanned spacecraft have landed on the Moon.

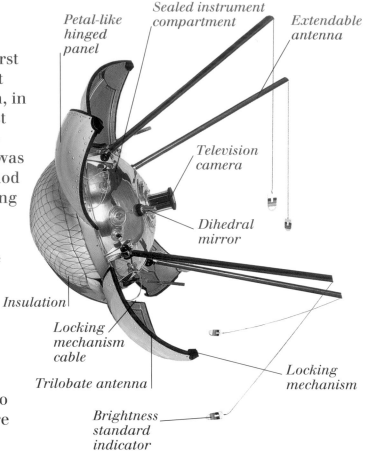

Petal-like hinged panel

Sealed instrument compartment

Extendable antenna

Television camera

Dihedral mirror

Insulation

Locking mechanism cable

Trilobate antenna

Locking mechanism

Brightness standard indicator

LUNOKHOD 1

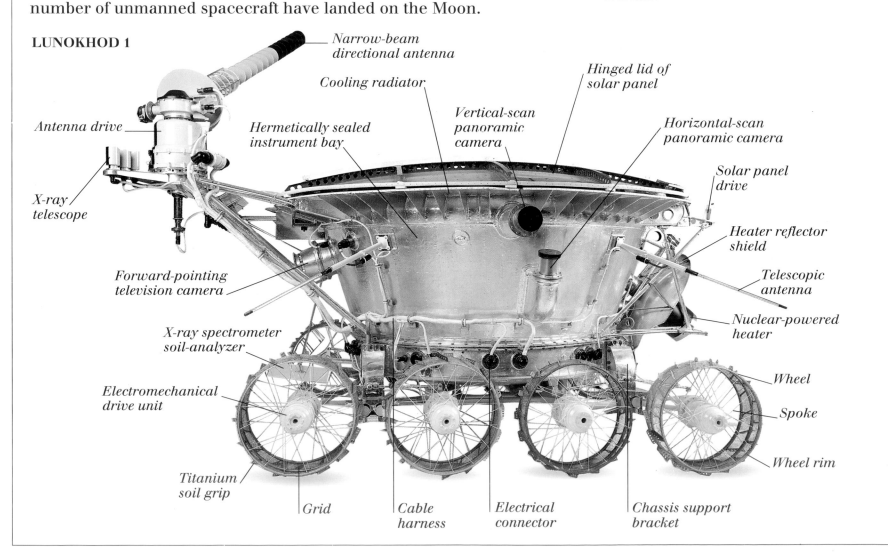

Narrow-beam directional antenna

Cooling radiator

Hinged lid of solar panel

Vertical-scan panoramic camera

Horizontal-scan panoramic camera

Antenna drive

Hermetically sealed instrument bay

Solar panel drive

X-ray telescope

Heater reflector shield

Forward-pointing television camera

Telescopic antenna

X-ray spectrometer soil-analyzer

Nuclear-powered heater

Electromechanical drive unit

Wheel

Spoke

Titanium soil grip

Wheel rim

Grid

Cable harness

Electrical connector

Chassis support bracket

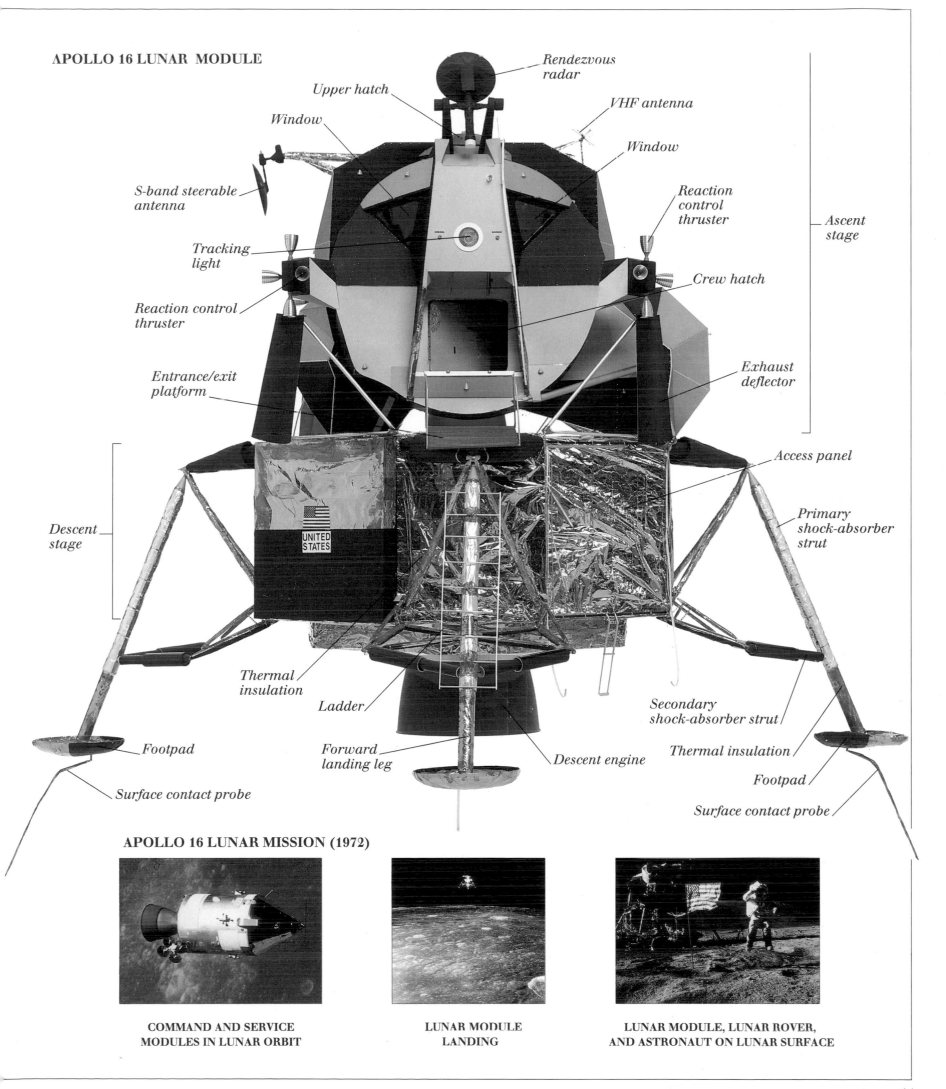

APOLLO 16 LUNAR MODULE

Rendezvous radar

Upper hatch

Window

VHF antenna

Window

S-band steerable antenna

Reaction control thruster

Ascent stage

Tracking light

Reaction control thruster

Crew hatch

Entrance/exit platform

Exhaust deflector

Access panel

Descent stage

Primary shock-absorber strut

Thermal insulation

Ladder

Secondary shock-absorber strut

Thermal insulation

Footpad

Forward landing leg

Descent engine

Footpad

Surface contact probe

Surface contact probe

APOLLO 16 LUNAR MISSION (1972)

COMMAND AND SERVICE MODULES IN LUNAR ORBIT

LUNAR MODULE LANDING

LUNAR MODULE, LUNAR ROVER, AND ASTRONAUT ON LUNAR SURFACE

Astronomical data 1

PLANETS OF THE SOLAR SYSTEM

Mercury Venus Earth Mars

Jupiter

Saturn

Uranus

Neptune

Pluto

PLANETS

	Mercury	Venus	Earth	Mars	Jupiter	Saturn	Uranus	Neptune	Pluto
Mass (Earth = 1)	0.055	0.81	1	0.11	318	95.18	14.5	17.14	0.0022
Equatorial diameter (miles)	3,031	7,521	7,926	4,217	88,850	74,901	31,765	30,777	1,429
Volume (Earth = 1)	0.056	0.86	1	0.15	1,323	744	67	57	unknown
Average density (g/cm³; water = 1g/cm³)	5.42	5.25	5.52	3.94	1.33	0.69	1.27	1.71	2.03
Equatorial surface gravity (Earth = 1)	0.38	0.86	1	0.38	2.5	1.1	1.1	1.1	unknown
Equatorial escape velocity (miles/sec)	2.7	6.4	7	3.1	37	22.1	13.2	14.7	0.7
Axial tilt (degrees)	2	2	23.4	24	3.1	26.7	97.9	28.8	57.5
Rotational period (length of day) (d = Earth day, h = Earth hour)	58.65d	243.01d*	23.93h	24.62h	9.92h	10.67h	17.23h*	16.12h	6.38d*
Average surface temperature (°F)	-270 to 800	867	59	-40	-180	-290	-350	-360	-360
Number of known rings	0	0	0	0	1	7	11	4	0
Number of moons	0	0	1	2	16	18	15	8	1
Maximum apparent magnitude	-1.4	-4.4	-	-2.8	-2.8	-0.3	5.5	7.8	13.6
Aphelion (million miles)	43.3	67.7	94.5	154.8	507	936	1,867	2,819	4,583
Perihelion (million miles)	28.5	66.7	91.4	128.4	460	837	1,700	2,769	2,750
Average distance from Sun (million miles)	36	67.2	93	141.6	483.6	887	1,783.2	2,794.2	3,666.3
Average orbital velocity (miles/sec)	29.8	21.8	18.5	15	8.1	6	4.2	3.4	2.9
Orbital tilt (degrees)	7	3.39	0	1.85	1.3	2.49	0.77	1.77	17.2
Orbital period (length of year) (y = Earth year, d = Earth day)	87.97d	224.7d	365.26d	1.88y	11.86y	29.46y	84.01y	164.79y	248.54y

*= rotation is retrograde

THE SUN

Approximate age (billion years)	4.6
Star type	Yellow main sequence
Mass (Earth = 1)	332,946
Equatorial diameter (miles)	869,900
Average density (g/cm³; water = 1g/cm³)	1.41
Apparent magnitude	-26.7
Absolute magnitude	4.83
Luminosity (billion billion megawatts)	390
Average surface temperature (°F)	9,900
Approximate core temperature (°F)	27,000,000
Maximum distance from Earth (miles)	94,500,000
Minimum distance from Earth (miles)	91,350,000
Average distance from Earth (miles)	93,000,000
Polar rotation period (Earth days)	35
Equatorial rotation period (Earth days)	25

FAMOUS COMETS

Name	Period (years)
D'Arrest's Comet	6.6
Encke's Comet	3.3
Comet Giacobini-Zinner	6.5
Great Comet of 1811	3,000
Great Comet of 1843	512.4
Great Comet of 1844	102,050
Great Comet of 1864	2,800,000
Halley's Comet	76.3
Holmes' Comet	6.9
Comet Kohoutek	75,000
Comet Mrkós	5.3
Olber's Comet	74
Pons-Winnecke Comet	6
Comet Schwassmann-Wachmann	16.2

COMET

MOONS

Name of planet	Name of moon	Diameter (miles)	Average distance from planet (miles)	Orbital period (Earth days)	Orbital tilt (degrees)
Earth	Moon	2,155	238,900	27.3	5.1
Mars	Phobos	14*	5,800	0.3	1.1
	Deimos	8*	14,600	1.4	1.8
Jupiter	Metis	25	79,500	0.3	0
	Adrastea	12*	80,000	0.3	0
	Amalthea	125	112,700	0.5	0.45
	Thebe	62*	137,900	0.7	0.9
	Io	2,263	262,100	1.8	0.04
	Europa	1,950	416,900	3.6	0.47
	Ganymede	3,270	664,900	7.2	0.21
	Callisto	2,983	1,168,200	16.7	0.51
	Leda	9	6,894,000	238.7	26.1
	Himalia	106	7,134,000	250.6	27.6
	Lysithea	22	7,283,000	259.2	29
	Elara	43	7,293,000	259	24.8
	Ananke	16	13,174,000	631	147
	Carme	25	14,044,000	692	164
	Pasiphae	37	14,603,000	735	145
	Sinope	25	14,727,000	758	153
Saturn	Pan	12	83,000	0.57	very small
	Atlas	19*	85,600	0.6	0.3
	Prometheus	63*	86,600	0.6	0
	Pandora	53*	88,100	0.6	0.1
	Epimetheus	73	94,100	0.7	0.3
	Janus	117*	94,100	0.7	0.1
	Mimas	247	115,600	0.9	1.52
	Enceladus	309	148,000	1.4	0.02
	Tethys	652	183,000	1.9	1.86
	Telesto	14*	183,000	1.9	unknown
	Calypso	15*	183,000	1.9	unknown
	Dione	695	234,000	2.7	0.02
	Helene	20*	234,000	2.7	0.2
	Rhea	949	327,000	4.6	0.35
	Titan	3,200	759,000	15.9	0.33
	Hyperion	178*	920,400	21.3	0.43
	Iapetus	892	2,213,000	79.3	14.7
	Phoebe	137	8,050,000	550.4	175
Uranus	Cordelia	16	30,900	0.3	very small
	Ophelia	20	33,400	0.4	very small
	Bianca	27	36,800	0.4	very small
	Cressida	41	38,400	0.5	very small
	Desdemona	36	39,000	0.5	very small
	Juliet	52	40,000	0.5	very small
	Portia	68	41,100	0.5	very small
	Rosalind	36	43,400	0.6	very small
	Belinda	42	46,800	0.6	very small
	Puck	96	53,400	0.8	very small
	Miranda	293	80,700	1.4	3.4
	Ariel	720	118,800	2.5	0
	Umbriel	726	165,300	4.1	0
	Titania	981	270,900	8.7	0
	Oberon	946	362,000	13.5	0
Neptune	Naiad	34	29,800	0.3	0
	Thalassa	50	31,100	0.3	0
	Despina	112	32,600	0.3	0
	Galatea	93	38,500	0.4	0
	Larissa	119	45,700	0.6	0
	Proteus	259	73,100	1.1	4.5
	Triton	1,681	220,500	5.9	160
	Nereid	186	3,426,000	360.2	27
Pluto	Charon	746	12,200	6.4	98.8

*= average diameter for irregularly shaped moon

THE MOON

TOTAL SOLAR ECLIPSES (UNTIL 2005)

Date	Where visible
November 3, 1994	Indian Ocean, South Atlantic, South America, Mid-Pacific.
October 24, 1995	Middle East, South Asia, South Pacific.
March 9, 1997	Siberia, Arctic.
February 26, 1998	Mid-Pacific, Central America, North Atlantic.
August 11, 1999	North Atlantic, North Europe, Middle East, North India.
June 21, 2001	South America, South Atlantic, Southern Africa, Pacific.
December 4, 2002	Mid-Atlantic, Southern Africa, South Pacific, Australia.
November 23, 2003	South Pacific, Antarctica.

TOTAL LUNAR ECLIPSES (UNTIL 2005)

Date	Where visible
November 29, 1993	North, South, and Central America.
April 4, 1996	Africa, Southeast Europe.
September 27, 1996	North, South, and Central America, West Africa.
September 16, 1997	Southern Africa, East Africa, Australia.
January 21, 2000	North, South, and Central America, Southwest Europe, West Africa.
July 16, 2000	Pacific, Australia, Southeast Asia.
January 9, 2001	Africa, Asia, Europe.
May 16, 2003	South and Central America, Antarctica.
November 9, 2003	North, South, and Central America.
May 4, 2004	Africa, Middle East, India.
October 28, 2004	North, South, and Central America, West Africa, South Europe.

Astronomical data 2

LOCAL GROUP OF GALAXIES

Name/Catalog number	Type	Distance (light-years)	Luminosity (million Suns)	Diameter (light-years)
Milky Way	Spiral	0	15,000	100,000
Large Magellanic Cloud	Irregular spiral	170,000	2,000	30,000
Small Magellanic Cloud	Irregular	190,000	500	20,000
Sculptor	Elliptical	300,000	1	6,000
Carina	Elliptical	300,000	0.01	3,000
Draco	Elliptical	300,000	0.1	3,000
Sextans	Elliptical	300,000	0.01	3,000
Ursa Minor	Elliptical	300,000	0.1	2,000
Fornax	Elliptical	500,000	12	6,000
Leo I	Elliptical	600,000	0.6	2,000
Leo II	Elliptical	600,000	0.4	2,000
NGC 6822	Irregular	1,800,000	90	15,000
IC 5152	Irregular	2,000,000	60	3,000
WLM	Irregular	2,000,000	90	6,000
Andromeda (M31)	Spiral	2,200,000	40,000	150,000
Andromeda I	Elliptical	2,200,000	1	5,000
Andromeda II	Elliptical	2,200,000	1	5,000
Andromeda III	Elliptical	2,200,000	1	5,000
M32 (NGC 221)	Elliptical	2,200,000	130	5,000
NGC 147	Elliptical	2,200,000	50	8,000
NGC 185	Elliptical	2,200,000	60	8,000
NGC 205	Elliptical	2,200,000	160	11,000
M33 (Triangulum)	Spiral	2,400,000	5,000	40,000
IC 1613	Irregular	2,500,000	50	10,000
DDO 210	Irregular	3,000,000	2	5,000
Pisces	Irregular	3,000,000	0.6	2,000
GR 8	Irregular	4,000,000	2	1,500
IC 10	Irregular	4,000,000	250	6,000
Sagittarius	Irregular	4,000,000	1	4,000
Leo A	Irregular	5,000,000	20	7,000
Pegasus	Irregular	5,000,000	20	7,000

SIDE VIEW OF OUR GALAXY
(THE MILKY WAY)

OVERHEAD VIEW OF OUR GALAXY
(THE MILKY WAY)

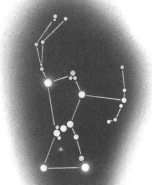

ORION

BRIGHTEST STARS

Name/Catalog number	Constellation	Apparent magnitude	Absolute magnitude	Distance (light-years)	Star type
Sun		-26.7	4.8	0.000015*	Yellow main sequence
Sirius A	Canis Major (The Great Dog)	-1.4	1.4	8.6	White main sequence
Canopus	Carina (The Keel)	-0.7	-8.5	1,200	White supergiant
Alpha Centauri A	Centaurus (The Centaur)	-0.1	4.1	4.3	Yellow main sequence
Arcturus	Boötes (The Herdsman)	-0.1	-0.3	37	Red giant
Vega	Lyra (The Lyre)	0.04	0.5	27	White main sequence
Capella	Auriga (The Charioteer)	0.1	-0.6	45	Yellow giant
Rigel	Orion (The Huntsman)	0.1	-7.1	540–900	White supergiant
Procyon	Canis Minor (The Little Dog)	0.4	2.7	11.3	Yellow main sequence
Achernar	Eridanus (River Eridanus)	0.5	-1.3	85	White main sequence

*= 93,000,000 miles

NEAREST STARS

Name/Catalog number	Constellation	Distance (light-years)	Apparent magnitude	Absolute magnitude	Star type
Sun		0.000015*	-26.7	4.8	Yellow main sequence
Proxima Centauri	Centaurus (The Centaur)	4.2	11	15.5	Red dwarf
Alpha Centauri A	Centaurus (The Centaur)	4.3	-0.1	4.1	Yellow main sequence
Alpha Centauri B	Centaurus (The Centaur)	4.3	1.4	5.7	Orange main sequence
Barnard's Star	Ophiuchus (The Serpent Bearer)	5.9	9.5	13	Red dwarf
Wolf 359	Leo (The Lion)	7.6	13.5	16.7	Red dwarf
Lalande 21185	Ursa Major (The Great Bear)	8.1	7.5	10.4	Red dwarf
Sirius A	Canis Major (The Great Dog)	8.6	-1.4	1.5	White main sequence
Sirius B	Canis Major (The Great Dog)	8.6	8.7	12	White dwarf
UV Ceti A	Cetus (The Whale)	8.9	12.4	15	Red dwarf

*= 93,000,000 miles

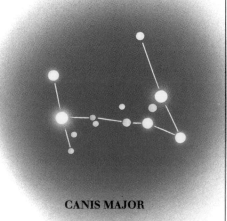

CANIS MAJOR

Glossary

ACCRETION DISK: A disk of material spiraling around an object, such as a black hole, due to gravity.

APHELION: The point farthest from the Sun in the orbit of a body around the Sun. (See also Perihelion.)

APOGEE: The point farthest from the Earth in the orbit of the Moon or an artificial satellite around the Earth. (See also Perigee.)

ASTEROID (MINOR PLANET): A small, rocky body orbiting the Sun, usually in the asteroid belt between Mars and Jupiter.

ASTRONOMICAL UNIT (AU): A unit of distance equal to the average distance between the Earth and the Sun: 92,955,807 miles.

ATMOSPHERE: The outer gaseous layer around a planet, moon, or star. It has no definite outer boundary and thins until it merges into space.

AXIS OF ROTATION: The imaginary line about which a body rotates. The **axial tilt** or **inclination** is the angle between the axis of rotation and the perpendicular to the orbital plane. (See also Orbit.)

BIG BANG THEORY: The theory that the Universe began when space, time, and matter came into being in a huge explosion (the Big Bang) between 10 and 20 billion years ago.

BINARY STAR: A pair of stars that orbit one another. About half of all known stars belong to groups of two or more.

BLACK HOLE: A region of space around a collapsed star where gravity is so strong that nothing, not even light, can escape. (See also Event horizon.)

CELESTIAL SPHERE: An imaginary hollow sphere on which, from the Earth, celestial objects appear to lie. The **celestial equator** is marked by the projection of the Earth's equator on to the celestial sphere. The **celestial poles** are the points on the celestial sphere above the Earth's north and south poles.

COMET: A small, icy body orbiting the Sun in a long, eccentric orbit.

CONSTELLATION: The pattern formed by a group of stars in the sky. The stars are not necessarily physically associated, since they may lie at different distances from the Earth.

DAY: The time taken for a planet to rotate once about its axis. A **sidereal day** is the time taken for a star to return to the same position in the sky. A **solar day** lasts from sunrise to sunrise.

DWARF STAR: A main sequence star (see Main sequence star).

ECLIPSE: The total or partial obscuring of one celestial body by another. In a **solar eclipse**, the Moon passes between the Sun and the Earth, hiding part or all of the Sun from a small area on Earth. In a **lunar eclipse**, the Earth comes between the Moon and the Sun, and the Moon passes through the Earth's shadow.

ECLIPTIC: The plane in which the Earth orbits around the Sun.

EVENT HORIZON: The boundary of a black hole. Light emitted from inside the event horizon cannot escape, so it is impossible to observe events occurring within it. (See also Black hole.)

GALAXY: A collection of stars, gas, and dust held together by gravity. Galaxies are classified as **spiral**, **elliptical**, or **irregular** according to their shape. They usually occur in groups known as **clusters**.

GIANT AND SUPERGIANT STARS: Large stars with a high luminosity. **Giants** are 10–1,000 times brighter than the Sun, with diameters 10–100 times greater. **Supergiants** are the largest and most luminous stars, thousands of times brighter and with diameters up to 1,000 times greater than the Sun.

GRAVITATION (GRAVITY): The attractive force between bodies, which depends on their mass and the distance between them. It holds less massive bodies in orbit around more massive ones, such as the planets around the Sun.

HERTZSPRUNG-RUSSELL DIAGRAM: A graph displaying the relationship between the luminosities and spectral types (colors) of stars. Other factors, such as stellar temperature, may also be included.

LIGHT-YEAR: A unit of distance equal to the distance traveled by light (or any electromagnetic radiation) through a vacuum in one year. One light-year is 5.88 million million miles, or 63,240 astronomical units, or 0.3066 parsecs. One **light-second** is 186,322 miles. (See also Astronomical unit; Parsec.)

LOCAL GROUP OF GALAXIES: The cluster of at least 28 galaxies to which our galaxy (the Milky Way Galaxy) belongs.

LUMINOSITY: The brightness of a luminous body, e.g., a star, defined by the total energy it radiates in a given time.

MAGNITUDE: A measurement of the brightness of a star or other celestial body. **Apparent magnitude** is the brightness of an object as seen from Earth. **Absolute magnitude** is the magnitude that an object would have if observed from a standard distance of 10 parsecs. (See also Luminosity.)

MAIN SEQUENCE STAR: A star that falls within a well-defined diagonal band on the Hertzsprung-Russell diagram. Main sequence stars produce energy by fusing hydrogen to form helium in their cores. (See also Hertzsprung-Russell diagram.)

METEOROID: A particle of dust or rock traveling through space at high speed. A **meteor** (also called a shooting star) is the streak of light seen when a meteoroid burns up in the Earth's atmosphere. A **meteorite** is a larger meteoroid that enters the atmosphere and reaches the surface of the Earth. **Meteor showers** occur when the Earth passes through a stream of debris in space.

MILKY WAY: The band of hazy light across the night sky coming from the multitude of stars in our galaxy.

MOON: A natural satellite of a planet. Also the name for the Earth's only natural satellite. (See also Satellite.)

NEBULA: A cloud of interstellar gas and dust. Nebulae are detectable as **emission nebulae**, which glow, **reflection nebulae**, which scatter starlight, and **dark nebulae**, which obscure light from more distant stars or nebulae.

NEUTRINO: An elementary particle with no electric charge and almost no mass, effectively traveling at the speed of light. Neutrinos very rarely interact with any other matter.

NEUTRON STAR: A stellar core that has collapsed until it consists almost entirely of neutrons. It has a mass between about 1.5 and 3 solar masses, but a very small diameter (typically about 6 miles). Neutron stars are detected as pulsars (see Pulsar).

ORBIT: The curved path of a body through space, influenced by the gravitational pull of a more massive body. The **orbital plane** is the plane in which the orbit lies. The **orbital tilt** is the angle between the orbital plane and a reference plane, e.g., the ecliptic. The **orbital period** is the time a body takes to complete one orbit. (See also Year; Ecliptic.)

PARSEC: A unit of distance equal to 3.26 light-years, or 206,265 astronomical units. (See also Astronomical unit; Light-year.)

PERIGEE: The point nearest the Earth in the orbit of the Moon or an artificial satellite around the Earth. (See also Apogee.)

PERIHELION: The point nearest the Sun in the orbit of a planet or other body around the Sun. (See also Aphelion.)

PHASES: The apparent changes in shape of the Moon and some planets as different amounts of their sunlit sides become visible from Earth.

PLANET: A relatively large body in orbit around the Sun or another star. Planets shine only by reflecting a sun's light.

PROTOSTAR: The earliest stage in the life of a star, during which it is condensing in a nebula but before it becomes a main sequence star.

PULSAR: A source of regularly pulsating radio waves (and sometimes light and other radiation). Pulsars are believed to be rotating neutron stars.

QUASAR (QUASI-STELLAR OBJECT): A compact, extremely luminous object that appears like a star when viewed from Earth. Little is known about quasars, but they are probably the nuclei of active galaxies, with supermassive black holes as their energy source.

RADIATION: Waves or particles emitted by a source. **Electromagnetic radiation** is energy traveling in the form of waves, including gamma rays, X-rays, ultraviolet radiation, visible light, infrared radiation, microwaves, and radio waves. **Particle radiation** includes elementary particles such as the protons and electrons in the solar wind.

RED DWARF: A small star with low surface temperature, and the faintest luminosity of all main sequence stars (see Main sequence star).

RETROGRADE MOTION: Backward motion, i.e., clockwise motion (viewed from above) of a body around the Sun, or of a moon around its planet, or of a planet around its axis of rotation.

RING SYSTEM: A thin disk of dust, rocks, or ice particles orbiting in the equatorial plane of some large planets.

SATELLITE: A body in orbit around a larger, parent body. **Natural satellites** of planets are called moons. **Artificial satellites** have been put into orbit around the Earth, the Moon, and some other planets. (See also Moon.)

SINGULARITY: A theoretical point or region in space-time where the laws of physics break down. Theory predicts a singularity with infinite density and pressure at the center of a black hole.

SOLAR SYSTEM: The Sun and all the bodies that orbit around it due to gravity.

SPECTRUM: A band or series of lines of electromagnetic radiation produced by splitting the radiation into its constituent wavelengths, e.g., the band of rainbow colors produced by splitting white light.

STAR: A luminous ball of gas that shines by generating energy in its core by nuclear reactions.

SUN: The central star of the Solar System. It is a main sequence star and is average in size and luminosity.

SUPERNOVA: The catastrophic explosion of a massive star at the end of its life, during which it may become as bright as a whole galaxy. A **supernova remnant** is the expanding cloud it leaves behind.

VARIABLE STAR: A star whose brightness varies.

WHITE DWARF: A small, very dense, collapsed star that is gradually cooling.

YEAR: The time taken for a planet to orbit the Sun once. A **sidereal year** is the time for one orbit measured using the fixed stars as a positional reference point. A **tropical year** is one orbit measured using a specific position of the Sun on the celestial sphere as a reference point. (See also Celestial sphere; Orbit.)

Index

Acknowledgments

Dorling Kindersley would like to thank:
John Becklake; the Memorial Museum of Cosmonautics, Moscow; the Cosmos Pavilion, Moscow; the U.S. Space and Rocket Center, Huntsville, Alabama; Broadhurst, Clarkson & Fuller Ltd

Special thanks to Susannah Massey (shoot-coordinator and translator) and to Gevorkyan Tatyana Alekseyevna, Leading Scientific Fellow and Historian of Cosmonautics (technical expert)

Picture research:
Catherine O'Rourke, Anna Lord

Picture credits:
The Planetarium, Armagh/Anglo-Australian Telescope Board 7car, 7cl, 7cbl, 8tr, 8b, 9tl, 9bl, 10tl, 12b, 13t, 13bl, 18tl; D. Malin 12tl, 22tr, 23tl; ESA/PLV 7bl; NASA/JPL 5cr, 7br, 26t, 26bl, 26br, 27bl, 30t, 36bl, 36cr, 40cr, 42crb, 44tr, 46bc, 48cr, 55bc, 55br, 55bl; NASA 40tl; Royal Observatory, Edinburgh/D. Malin 7tl, 7cr, 8c, 12cl, 12cr, 13br; Tom Van Sant/Geosphere

Project, Santa Monica/Science Photo Library 34 cl, 34cr; Duncan Brown 2l, 52b; Geoff Dann 51b; Jet Propulsion Laboratory 7cbr, 26bc, 27bc, 27bcr, 34tl, 38crb, 40cb, 40cbr, 40bc, 40br, 42tl, 42cr, 42cb, 42bc, 42br, 46tl, 46cra, 46cl, 46c, 46cr, 46br, 51tr, 51cr, 52tl, 54tl; The Lund Observatory 11b; National Optical Astro Observatory 48tr; Science Photo Library 6bl, 24t; Jodrell Bank 2cr, 7tr, 9c; Hale Observatories 28br; Dr. William C. Keel 9br; Denis Milon 48bl; NASA 7cal, 8tl, 11tr, 26c, 27br, 28t, 30cr, 31tl, 32tl, 32cr, 32cl, 32b, 38cr, 38br, 48tl; NASA/AUI 9tr; Novosti Press Agency 38bc; David Parker 50tl; Max Planck Institute for Radio Astronomy 11tl; Rev. Ronald Royer 28cr; U.S. Geological Survey/Science Photo Library 3, 26bcr, 38tl, 38bl; Floor of the Oceans, by Bruce C. Heezen and Marie Tharp 1975. © Marie Tharp 1980. Reproduced by permission of Marie Tharp, 1 Washington Ave, South Nyack, NY 10960, USA 34b. **Jacket:** The Planetarium, Armagh/Anglo-Australian Telescope Board; NASA/JPL; Jet Propulsion Laboratory; Science Photo Library/NASA; Max Planck Institute for Radio Astronomy; U.S. Geological Survey
(t=top, b=bottom, a=above, l=left, r=right, c=center)